SPINNING AND WEAVING

Spinning and Weaving

DRAKE PUBLISHERS INC   New York

Acknowledgements

Pages 2, 9, 37 and 51 designed and created by April Bamford.
Front cover and page 65. Poncho cape
by courtesy of the NZ Wool Board.

All photographs supplied by Richard Silcock

ISBN 0-87749-324-3

LCCCN 72-10515

Published in 1973 by
Drake Publishers Inc
381 Park Avenue South
New York, N.Y. 10016

Printed in Taiwan

Contents

Spinning & weaving

The combined craft of spinning and weaving ranks among the grand crafts. Man functions most creatively when his very existence is at stake. Early weavers wove their fabrics in order to continue to live. In the same way that the potters of pre-history built pots to hold stew, the weavers of that era wove cloth to keep warm.

Much as we may personally deplore undue emphasis on history, we cannot ignore the racial memories which have come to us with our ancestry. Weaving, born of necessity in the pre-conscious period of our racial history, retains a very special place in the human urge to make and create.

It is for this reason, as much as for any other, that spinning and weaving offers craftsmen of today the satisfaction of using their hands, their eyes, their creative endeavours to some purpose. Honest utilitarianism in creating an object of use as well as of beauty, is the basis of much of the increasing popularity of the twin crafts of spinning and weaving.

It is almost a secondary consideration that weavers obtain from their craft completely exclusive fabrics that put to shame the weaving quality of any comparable factory-made material. These advantages are an additional bonus granted in addition to the creative satisfaction of spinning and weaving.

As this book will prove, neither spinning nor weaving are expensive crafts in which to engage. Certainly, quantity production of fabric, spun from the raw fibre and woven into cloth, requires some outlay in equipment but it is a mistake to believe that excellent garments cannot be made unless an expensive loom and spinning wheel are first purchased. On the contrary, this book is expressly designed to allow folk who may be interested in spinning and weaving to first make garments beginning with the raw wool before deciding to spend money, or time in providing themselves with elaborate equipment. Also included in the book is information for experienced weavers to assist them to extend their mastery of their craft.

In particular, the book is aimed towards the use of creative imagination in the art of weaving; towards the extension of each weaver's creativity toward full self-expression, so making their weaving an individualistic craft and not, as too often happens, the slavish mechanical following of something developed by somebody else.

CHAPTER ONE

Wool

Wool is nature's wonder fibre. Despite man's ingenuity and technological progress man-made fibres have not even approached the versatility and sheer use value of wool. Wool fibre is a highly complex material, so complex that it includes in its structure attributes bewildering in their variety. No man-made fibre can both shed water and yet absorb perspiration; wool accomplishes this. None of wool's competitors has at the one time high thermal insulating properties, considerable resistance to wear, great natural beauty as well as softness to the touch. Springiness and the ability to drape may be allied characteristics, but wool fabrics possess these in greater measure than do fabrics made from any other fibre.

Wool, laid down molecule by molecule in the wool follicle of a sheep's skin, will continue to be the basis for the highest quality cloth and upholstery fabrics, for the longest wearing, most luxurious carpeting and the most comfortable of clothing from the tropics to the arctic, from the working man in the field and mine to the debutante in the ballroom. So far ahead of all other materials does wool lead the field that to spend time and creative endeavour on lesser weaving threads is unworthy of one's talent.

Wool for weaving

The price differential that exists between raw wool in the form of fleece wool as shorn from the sheep and prepared wool as sold by craft shops for weaving and rug making is very great. In addition natural fleece wool handled by a craftsman and subject to less arduous treatment than factory processed wool yields a thread that is more wear resistant than any machine treated wool.

Factory processing need not, but almost invariably does, remove the natural oil from wool. The greater part of the natural wool oil is lanolin, a constituent in many toilet preparations and to lose this is to make the wool less pliable and hence less long-wearing and less able to shed water. Weaving is a time-consuming craft justified by the considerable enjoyment derived both in the creation of a worthwhile fabric and in the pride of possession of the finished article. As the joy to be found in weaving reflects the quality of production, and in consideration of the time that must be spent, it seems reasonable to extend both the time and the enjoyment to producing one's own homespun wool.

If any further justification is needed for urging that homecrafters weave from their own home-spun, it can be taken into account that spinning by wheel is urged by many therapeutists as one of the most soothing of all occupations for the relief of overstrung nerves and the release of the tensions of modern life.

Choice of fleece

There is a great variation in the quality and characteristics of the wool grown by different breeds of sheep. So numerous are the different breeds of modern sheep that it is quite impossible to name them all here, yet alone give any indication of the characteristics of the wool of each breed. Yet some knowledge of the type of wool bought in the fleece is needed by a spinner if a reasonable choice of wool for a particular job is to be made. For this reason, a limited number of the more representative breeds are discussed at the end of this chapter, in order that fleece wool can be selected in the way a farmer or wool-broker will recognise. It must be realised that a variation in the fineness of wool can occur within a breed and by no means all wool will come from sheep that are purebred or even true to type. Despite this it will be possible to much more intelligently discuss fleece wool with a seller if some knowledge of fleece wool is known.

Characteristics of wool
Certain technical terms are commonly used in discussing wool. A few should be known by a weaver:

Wool terms for spinners
BREAK: A weak place in the staple due to a sudden thinning of fibres. Invariably caused by a sudden check to the growth of the fibre.
CANARY COLOUR: A yellow stain in wool which is not completely removed in scouring. Avoid using this.
CHARACTER: "Character" in wool means a combination of expressions, qualities or peculiarities which when considered in combination serve to distinguish the wools of different breeds.
COARSE: Usually synonymous with strong. Sometimes used to mean coarse handling.
COTTED WOOL: Wools in which fibres have become felted together.
CONDITION: Refers to the amount of non-wool constituents, such as yolk, sand, earth, etc., present in greasy wool.
COUNT: Refers only to yarn; is the number given to yarn to indicate the number of hanks per lb of yarn. Often synonymous with quality number.
CROSSBRED WOOL: Lustre wool varying in fineness from 36's to 56's irrespective of breed or cross.
CRIMPS: Natural undulations along the wool fibres.
FREE: With reference to wool usually means free of seeds, burr, etc. Sometimes means that fibres are free, i.e. not cotted.
FLEECE: The coat of one sheep.
GREASY WOOL: Wool in its natural condition as shorn from the sheep.
HANDLE: The quality of wool as judged by touch.
LONG WOOLS: Breeds of sheep which grow long and lustrous wools.
Lincoln English/Leicester Romney.
LUSTRE: The property by which wool reflects light. A characteristic of most coarse wools.

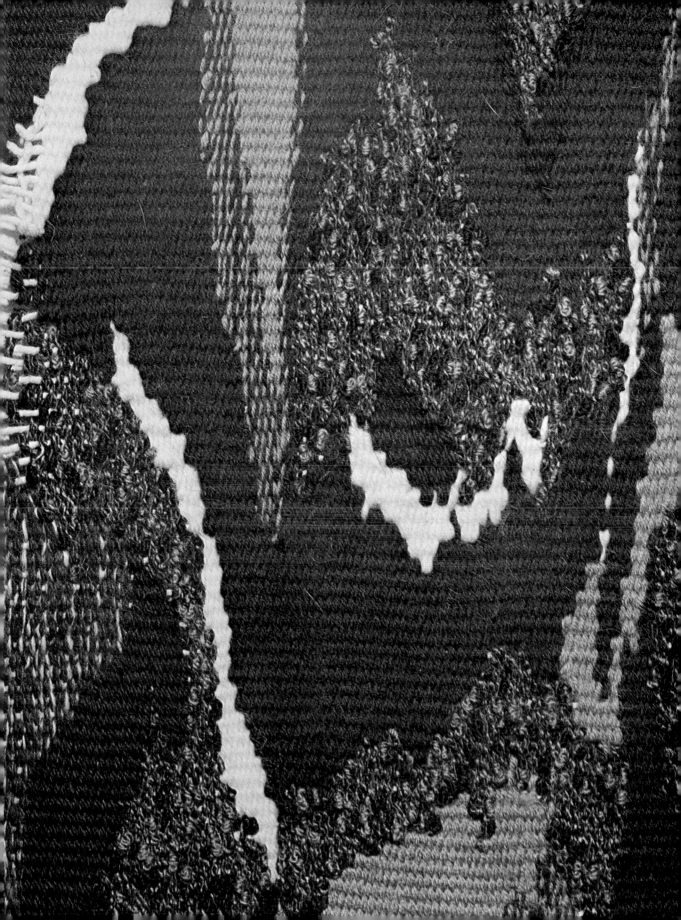

QUALITY (number): Refers to the fineness of wool which is relative and is indicated by an arbitrary number which originally had reference to the spinning value of the wool.

SOUND: An evenly grown wool of sufficient tensile strength throughout the staple.

STAPLES: Wool fibres generally show a marked characteristic tendency to grow in bunches, groups or clusters known as staples or locks.

STRONG: With reference to wool means coarse.

STYLE: A term broadly used to embrace characters, colour, condition, soundness, etc. The degree of style being indicated by such adjectives as super, average, inferior, or by letters such as A, BB, B, C or D.

SUINT: The secretion of the sweat glands of sheep.

TENDER: A wool deficient in tensile strength for much of its length.

TYPE: Refers to the characteristics which distinguish wools within breed as well as between breed, e.g. down, type, fine merino types, etc.

VIRGIN WOOL OR NEW WOOL: Wool which has not previously been manufactured.

YIELD: The weight of clean wool of normal condition (moisture content) expressed as per cent of the weight of greasy wool.

Testing wool for spinning

There is a lot of work required in the spinning and weaving of wool by hand and a good product will not come from poor raw material. Be firm when purchasing wool, remembering that the odd fleece of wool left lying around a farmer's property after shearing has finished for the season is liable to have been taken from a sheep that has died. Discuss the fleece with the farmer and note the points mentioned in the section immediately above. Test the wool by withdrawing several locks from different parts of the fleece and process as follows:

(1) Stretch the wool between the two hands, noting the spring.

(2) Give a sharp tug. If the majority of fibres part at approximately the same place discard the whole fleece. This is wool break and the wool is second grade or lower.

(3) With the lock stretched taut, flick with a finger. Good wool will twang. Any tendency for the wool to fray is a sign of rotten or dead wool.

It is wise to anticipate one's yearly needs and purchase the needed number of fleeces at a time when the shearing season is at its height. It is possible to buy raw wool from a number of sources away from the farm but there is something rather special in purchasing wool at the place where it was grown.

11

Home-spun processes
The making of threads for weaving is undertaken in four separate phases:

(1) Teasing and if necessary, oiling the wool.
(2) Carding and the making of "rolags". (Rolags being the bundles of wool, combed out and ready to be fed into the rotating section of the spinning wheel.)
(3) Spinning the wool.
(4) Plying two or more threads together.

Preparing the fleece wool
Unless the fleece is dirty and stained, it is not necessary to wash the wool before spinning. Dry mud and loose dirt will come away from the wool strands while teasing and if washing can be avoided, so much the better. Retaining the natural oil in the wool leaves it much easier to manipulate and much less likely to break during spinning. If washed, the oil has to be replaced, this is done during teasing. Olive oil may be rubbed into the hands during the teasing operation and this will be transferred to the wool. A slightly more efficient method is to make up the emulsion, the recipe for which is given directly below, and feed it regularly onto the wool being teased. This does allow a rather more even spread than through oiling the hands, but the commonsense arrangement seems to be to leave the oil in the wool in the first place and if necessary, wash the wool after spinning.

Oil emulsion for wool
> Olive oil – – – – – – – 4 parts
> Household ammonia (ammonium hydroxide) – 1 part
> Water – – – – – – – 2 parts
> Warm the mixture very slightly. Place in a loosely corked bottle (it is important that the cork be easily freed in case a pressure of ammonia gas builds up) and shake well. Fit with a sprinkler top.

The fleece should be laid flat, possibly on the floor but certainly on a large flat surface. Sort the parts carefully. The belly wool, the sides and other lesser parts of the fleece should be put aside. All tufts, hairy and stained pieces should be removed. The main body of the fleece is now ready for teasing.

Teasing wool

(1) A handful of wool is withdrawn from the fleece, care being taken not to disturb the lay of the fleece. In other words, care should be taken not to tangle the wool and this is another disadvantage of washing before spinning.
(2) Hold in the left hand and with the right hand draw away small pieces for the full length of the staple.
(3) The teasing operation should be done with a smooth, non-jerky motion and the teased wool should end up fluffy but retain some semblance of order.

It is during this operation that oil can be added if necessary. There are three ways in which this can be done:

(1) The teasing done with oil liberally applied to the hands. The teased wool is then laid aside for several days in a dry, warm place so the oil may penetrate all the fibres.
(2) The fleece, after sorting, but before teasing, is sprinkled with the oil water emulsion, rolled very tightly into a plastic bag and left in the warmth for a day or two.
(3) Very dense, very strongly crimped wool, even when not washed, is improved by taking out the locks separately (a lock of wool is formed by the natural parting of the fleece), oiling the tips of the fibres and carding immediately.

12

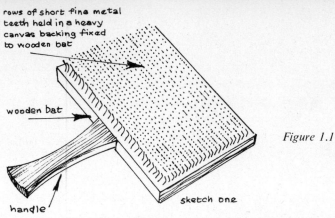

rows of short fine metal teeth held in a heavy canvas backing fixed to wooden bat

wooden bat

handle

card. (two required)

Figure 1.1

sketch one

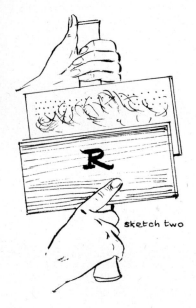

sketch two

In cool weather, the teasing should be done in a warm room in which the fleece has been left for sufficient length of time to reach room temperature. The teased wool can then be "carded" as explained in the next section.

Carding wool

The term carding refers to the loose rope (rolags) formed by using two pieces of apparatus called "Cards". This operation is shown in *Figure 1.1* and explained in the text below but while the use of cards is essential in order to speedily handle a quantity of wool, small quantities can be prepared for spinning in this way.

(1) A quantity of teased wool is taken, rolled between the hands until a loose roll some four or five inches long is formed.

(2) On the bare thigh the left hand rolls the wool backward and forward in such a way that the roll tends to work to the outside of the thigh. At the same time the right hand feeds more teased wool from the inside of the thigh, under the left hand.

(3) To make up rolags for later spinning, the roll is left very loose, but it should also be noted that continued rolling under pressure can and will produce quite long thin threads of wool. With some little practice, such threads can be made thin enough, firm enough and of sufficient length to be used either in weaving or in hand knitting. However, such thread is painstakingly made and is not as strong as spun thread.

The more conventional carding is carried out as follows (refer *Figure 1.1*):

Sketch 1: A card is a small wooden bat to which is affixed a canvas carrying a large number of fine wire teeth. The cards are used to straighten the strands of wool fibres by means of a combing action, prior to being spun. Cards or carders come in pairs and one should be marked right-hand and one left-hand. It is important that the right and left hand carders be used only in those hands, for after use the teeth acquire a "set" in the direction appropriate to the hand in which they are used. Cards are inexpensive and readily obtainable at craft shops. If difficulty is found in buying cards, a smaller, almost identical tool is sold by tool merchants under the label of "file cards".

In using cards, the operation is made much simpler if the placing of the hands on the card handles is convenient. Attention should be given to this point in the next three sketches, as with the correct placing of the hands, the correct movement automatically follows.

Sketch 2: The movements which lead to the operation depicted in this sketch follow each other thus:

(1) Sit down on a bench or other seat which does not impede free movement of the arms. Place the left card on the left knee with the teeth up.

(2) Pick up a small quantity of teased wool in the right hand and with a sweeping movement, spread it more or less across the left card.

14

(3) With the right-hand card, comb gently across the left card from left to right. The wool has now transferred from one card to the other.

Sketch 3: Transfer the wool back to the left card in this way:

(4) Raise the cards to a vertical position with handles upmost and hands held in the position shown.
(5) Place the upper edge of the left card to the lower edge of the right card.
(6) Draw the left card over the right. Repeat several times.
Remove the fleece from the cards by proceeding thus:
(7) Again raise the handles to the vertical position.
(8) Use the outside hooks of the right card as a comb to collect the wool on the outside edge of the right card.

Sketch 4: The action is transferred from the front of the card to the back and rolled into a rolag as follows:

(9) Use the back edge of the left card to roll the wool around the outside edge of the right card. The first few times this is tried the roll of wool falls to the ground but a little practice leads to proficiency. The secret is a clean, quick, sweeping movement.
(10) Roll several times between the backs of the two cards to form a rolag.

The wool is now ready for spinning which is discussed in the next chapter. Although the operations described have taken long in the telling, none of them are other than simple and with some practice can all be done very quickly. As with more repetitive tasks, the secret of making the task less bothersome and quick to carry out, is to make all movements rhythmical. This is specially important with carding where a rhythmical set of actions can make the rolags come from the cards in a constant stream.

A side benefit arising from the handling of raw wool is the wonderful pliability and softness that the lanolin of the wool gives to one's hands. This, plus the feeling one finds in appreciating what a wonderful substance wool is, does much to make the operation of preparing wool, a very pleasant and a very soothing occupation.

Selecting wool for hand spinning

It is possible to spin any type of wool provided there is enough length of fibre to handle into the spinner. Some wools are easier to spin than others and in general the coarser fibre wools spin more easily than the fine wools. However, it is a matter of practice and personal ability.

In order to select the type of wool you must know how to describe the fleece that you want to the supplier, using the right trade terms and descriptions.

Wools are described largely by the sheep that produce them with further details of the fibre diameter called 'count' or sometimes called

'quality'. (The word 'quality' must not be confused with style as in wool trade quality only means measurement of fibre diameter and not the assessment of the material. Style on the other hand refers to the characteristics of fibre in consideration of length, crimping, colour and strength.)

The following wools are generally available and should be asked for by name when ordering your spinning wool:

Merino Wool – This is an extra fine wool and has a silky texture and normally shows style but is often hard to spin by an inexperienced person because it is short in staple length and very fine to handle. It makes a beautiful soft thin yarn and is used for super fine and high quality materials.

Halfbred Wools – This is wool derived from the crossing of the Merino sheep and another long wool breed and is coarser and generally longer in the staple than Merino and is classed as fine wool.
Corridale – This is a halfbred wool showing generally good length and style and is one of the best spinning wools in the fine wool category.

Romney Type of Wool – This is a common type of crossbred wool and in general is a popular hand spinning wool provided that it is carefully chosen for its length, strength and style. It varies greatly in fibre diameter and has to be selected according to the type of yarn which you wish to spin. It is not classed as a fine wool and can be put into more than one category: That is coarse, medium and fine crossbred.

There are other crossbred type wools very similar to Romney as they are derived from crossing of Romney with other sheep such as the Cheviot, the Leicester, and the Lincoln, which give further variations of crossbred type spinning wools. These variations are such things as lustre, brightness, harshness, hairiness, and different fibre and staple formation.

Leicester Type Wool – These are generally coarser and more lustrous but often soft and easier to spin than the crossbred wools.

Lincoln Type Wool – These are again coarser and more lustrous than the Leicester and produce a very strong thick yarn and are fairly difficult to spin, but have the advantage of being very long and strong and make up good warp yarns.

When asking for wool use these terms and add further description of count and style as follows:

Merino Wool – 64's/70's or 70's/74's, good style colour and length. This will give you a super but very fine type of wool which probably only the expert spinners can use to advantage.
Halfbred Wool (*including Corridale*) – Ask for 56's/58's. This will give you a medium fine spinning wool.
Crossbred Wool – You can ask for three main ranges, 46's/48's, 48's/50's and 50's/52's. This will give you a range of coarser longer and easier spun wools.

Rev. Dr. Edmund Cartwright - inventor of power loom and woolcombing machine.

Leicester and Lincoln Type Wool – The count range is from 36's/46's. The Lincoln being in the range of 36's/40's and the Leicester in the range 40's/46's. This will give you 'strong' spinning types of wool. The word 'strong' refers here to the coarseness or thickness of the fibre and it is a trade term. Wools are referred to as being strong, medium, fine and extra fine, these terms being by the breeds already given above.

In general it is hard to hand spin any wool no matter how coarse, medium or fine which is less than $2\frac{1}{2}''$ in length of staple, therefore you should sort out shorter wool and discard it as being of little spinning value and probably a waste of time and money.

16

The above list barely touches on the very large number of sheep breeds available. Despite the number of omissions, it does contain a representative spread of wool types and if when buying wool an unknown breed is mentioned, the seller can be asked to relate the breed to one of the above breeds when the characteristics can be compared.

The choice of wool for spinning and weaving must be governed by the end use of the article being made. That is one of the great advantages of doing it one's self, the raw material can be chosen to match the use to which the manufactured article is to be put. Long staple, coarser wools will stand a tremendous amount of hard wear and have in full measure the outstanding characteristic of wool, the ability to be self-cleaning. Upholstery material, for instance, could be advantageously produced from a wool with a count of from 45's to 54's. Carpets and rugs are woven from fleeces with a count closer to 40's, while material which must be pleasant to the touch, such as that from which scarves are made, should be in the shorter stapled range from say 60's upwards.

All the above discussion neglects the possibility of blending wool, say a hard handle wool to give wearing quality and the spring necessary for good drape as required for formal wear and hangings, with a softer short staple wool which will tend to fill out the hard handle and make the material more pleasant to touch.

In dealing with natural wool, it should be remembered that fleeces can be obtained self-coloured in virtually all shades of white, cream, fawn, brown and black. It is possible, in many cases desirable, to knit or weave patterns into garments using no other colour than the natural colour of the wool as it comes from the sheep. It is fairly obvious that farmers attempt to breed odd colours out of their flocks but, much to the disgust of the owner, any sizable flock will throw black, brown and fawn lambs among the multitude of snowy off-springs. An arrangement with a farmer or wool broker may guarantee a steady supply of such coloured wool if a weaver will go to the trouble of seeking out such folk.

It may also be noted that wool from lambs differs entirely from that of adult sheep of the same breed and this further increases the range of textural variety which may be introduced into a weaving pattern by changes in the type of wool from which the thread is made.

No apology is made for the length of a chapter dealing only with the subject of wool. The choice of raw material is at least as important as any other aspect of spinning and weaving and far too many weavers have not realised, let alone exploited, the full benefits in textural and colour changes which can be brought about in their weaving by selecting the original fleece with this in mind. Both spinning and weaving are creative crafts, but only when imagination is brought to the application of artistic endeavour. Lack the necessary knowledge to create for one's self, and both spinning and weaving can become sterile mechanical chores, instead of proving the real joy of making and creating.

CHAPTER TWO

Spinning

Wool into thread is the purpose of spinning. In the beginning, to spin was to continue to exist. Every family in the days of our remote ancestors had their own spinners; cloth was a necessity. Then with greater organization and the specialization of the tasks of living, spinners and weavers had time to become artists, until by the Medieval period manufacturers of velvets, brocades, cloth of gold and fine woollens were honoured as great artist craftsmen. This was the supreme era of fine home-spun, magnificent hand-woven fabrics, with every piece offered in the great markets, an individual artistic creation. These super cloths and tapestries were not for the common folk. The lowlier sections of the community had to wait for the introduction of mechanised spinning and mechanical weaving before they too could wear as commonplace, fresh, reasonable quality fabric clothing.

Nobody would decry today the advantages of plentiful, low priced fabric but with the introduction of standardised products, there departs from the world the individuality, the freshness, the difference that exists in the creations of the highly skilled hand-craftsman. It is in the return to self-expression by the individual, the release of that artistic creativity within us, that hand spinning and hand weaving have such a mighty appeal.

Weaving with home-spun is entirely complementary to hand weaving and no true weaver should deny themselves the thrill of producing cloth which they themselves have created from wool as it came from the sheep's back. The slightly irregular thread size of home-spun in the cloth produces a pleasure to the eye and hand, unmatched by the mechanical regularity of machine spun thread. All this in addition to the considerable saving in cost of raw wool against prepared wool, and the longer life of home-spun as against machine spun.

Spinning wool
Wool can be spun to thread in three ways at home:

(1) By the method of hand rolling (in Chapter 1) where the making of rolags on the bare thigh is described. This can be satisfactory if great care is taken, but it requires very considerable patience and it is difficult to control the thread thickness. Hand rolling thread cannot be recommended except as a starting point to produce the thread for one or two garments.
(2) By the use of the 'Spindle', the most ancient of all spinning instruments. A simple device as shown in *Figure 2.1*, a satisfactory spindle can readily be made at home. Again, the use of a spindle is shown in *Figure 2.2* and explained below. There is also available on the market an ideal kit-set containing all the necessary instructions and materials for starting from the raw wool provided with the kit and ending with a comfortable, warm and essentially practical knitted garment, the thread being spun on a spindle included with the kit-set. It is a very wise move for a beginner to try out spindle spinning first. In this way a crafter can determine the personal appeal of spinning before investing in a comparatively expensive spinning wheel.

Figure 2.1

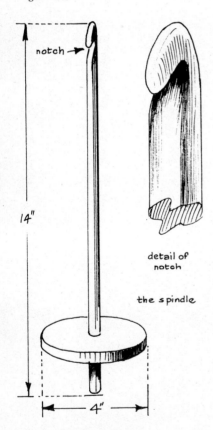

notch →

detail of notch

the spindle

14"

4"

sketch one

(3) By spinning on a wheel. The spinning wheel is the way to quantity production of home-spun. Worked by foot power in a soothing rhythm, both hands are free to feed and control the rolags into the spinning head.

Figure 2.4 depicts a spinning wheel and explains the use of the various parts. The operation of setting up a wheel and producing thread from it is explained later in this chapter.

The spindle
Refer *Figure 2.1*. A spindle is a smooth wooden stick to which is fitted a wooden disc about one inch from the lower end of the stick. A notch is cut in the stick (as shown in detail in the figure) about half an inch from the upper end. The way in which thread is spun is as follows: (See *Figure 2.2*)

(1) Take two feet in length of woollen thread, (machine made thread will do if it is soft and thick). One end of this thread is fastened in a double hitch around the shaft of the spindle just above the disc. See *Detail B*.
(2) The thread passes over the edge of the disc, is fastened around the bottom of the shaft in a hitch, and is brought up over the edge of the disc diametrically opposite the position where it passed downwards. Refer *Detail C*.
(3) The thread is now placed in the further notch at the upper end of the shaft and held there with a half hitch. This is shown in *Detail A*.

The spindle will now hang upright, suspended from the thread and can be spun by twisting between fingers and thumb to impart a twist to the thread from which it is hanging. This motion of the right hand to set the spindle spinning should be practiced a few times. Further operations are shown in *Sketch 2*.

Sketch 2
(1) The thread is cut within 2 or 3 inches of the top of the spindle.
(2) The end of the thread is well teased out.
(3) A rolag of wool is laid over the back of the left hand with some of the wool held between the finger and thumb of that hand.
(4) The teased loose end of the thread on the spindle is laid alongside the rolag between finger and thumb.
(5) The right hand imparts a fast spinning motion to the spindle.

All the above points are set out clearly in *Detail D*.

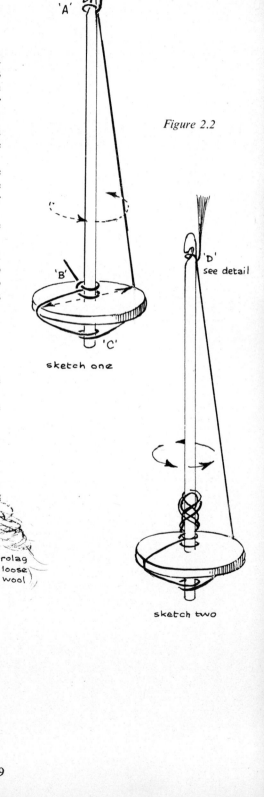

Figure 2.2

sketch one

sketch two

twist →

rolag
loose
wool

detail at 'D'

thread

19

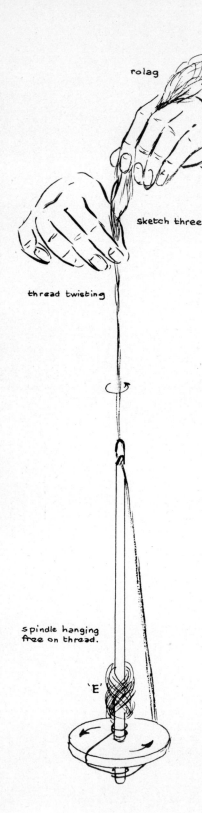

rolag

sketch three

thread twisting

spindle hanging
free on thread.

'E'

Figure 2.2

Sketch 3

(1) The right hand releases the spindle to spin free.

(2) The thread will begin to twist between the finger and thumb; pressure should be released just sufficiently to allow this twist to run between the finger and thumb and pick up the loose wool of the rolag with the teased end of the thread.

(3) As yarn is formed by the twisting motion of the thread pulling the loose wool into the thread, the formed yarn is allowed to pull out from between finger and thumb, so extending the length of the thread and lowering the spindle towards the floor.

(4) The right hand feeds additional rolags to the left hand as required, so keeping up the continuous production of thread.

One twist of the spindle should be sufficient to provide enough spin to take the spindle to the floor. The rolag wool should be held fairly tightly in the left hand so that no twist runs back to the loose wool on the back of the hand. It will be noted that the left hand does all the forming of the thread, the right hand acting as the assistant in a manner of speaking. A left-handed spinner may find it more convenient to reverse hands.

(5) When the spindle reaches the floor, the thread is slipped out of the notch and off the bottom of the shaft and wound onto the shaft of the spindle above the disc.

(6) The method of winding the spare thread onto the shaft is shown as *Detail E.* This is in the form of a figure eight as commonly used on fishing and kite lines. It is important that the greater weight of thread be kept near the disc so that the spindle will continue to spin true, without wobbling.

(7) A sufficient length of thread is left to reset the spindle and the above procedure is repeated until the amount of thread on the spindle becomes unwieldy.

Sketch 4

(1) When the spindle is full, the thread is eased up the shaft and the double hitch against the disc cut.

(2) A paper spill (or a number of paper spills) is made by rolling stiff paper into a tight roll to a diameter rather less than the diameter of the spindle shaft and fastening the loose end by binding with thread or even better with plastic tape.

(3) The loosened wool is slipped off the shaft directly onto the paper spill and put to one side ready for skeining, as explained at the end of this chapter.

The process of spinning with a spindle may appear complicated from the description but this is misleading for it is essentially a very simple operation. Surprisingly enough, it produces thread much quicker than one would suppose from the written discussion and it does not require a great deal of practice to become proficient and speedy in its use.

20

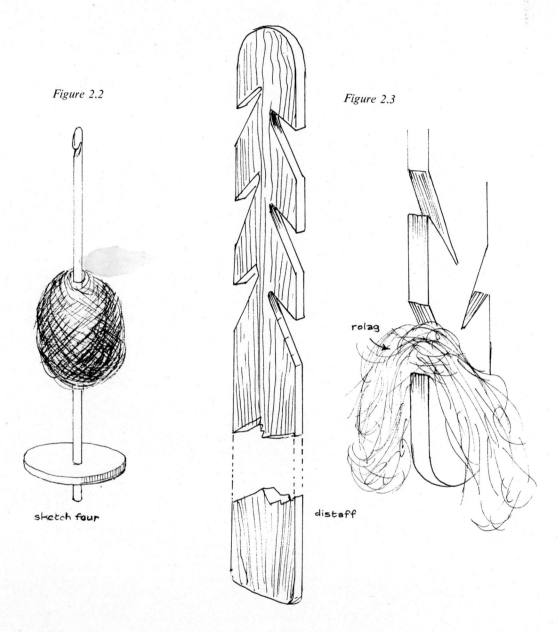

Figure 2.2

Figure 2.3

sketch four

rolag

distaff

The Distaff

The age-old symbol of the female side of the family, the distaff also symbolises the importance of spinning in past centuries. There is nothing esoteric about a distaff or the way it is used. In its simplest form it is merely a flat notched stick (as shown in *Figure 2.3*) on which rolags are carried. Placed in the belt or tucked under the arm, a distaff provided a convenient supply of rolags to enable spinning to continue while the 'distaff woman' (the female spinner) moved about her task of supervising the lesser servants or minding the children. There is little doubt of the advantages of a readily available supply of rolags while spindle spinning, and a distaff is a decided convenience.

21

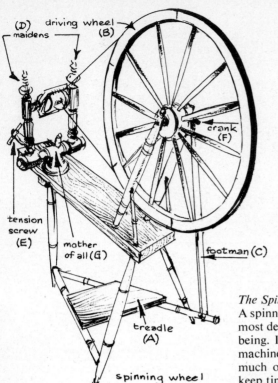

(D) maidens
driving wheel (B)

crank (F)

tension screw (E)

mother of all (G)

footman (C)

Figure 2.4

treadle (A)

spinning wheel

The Spinning Wheel

A spinning wheel in its traditional form is probably the smoothest running, most delightfully balanced machine ever designed to be driven by a human being. It is no wonder that spinners, soothed by the busy hum of their machines, have waxed poetic in the praise of their wheel and set to music much of this verse, to produce a great number of 'spinning songs' to keep time to the rhythmic movement of their hands and feet.

However, spinning wheels are most functional pieces of equipment, each part of which serves a useful purpose even though given some fanciful names. A typical horizontal type spinning wheel is diagrammed in *Figure 2.4*. There is also a vertical type similar in most respects to the one shown except that the spinning head is set above the driving wheel. The action of a spinning wheel can be seen by reference to *Figure 2.4* and the following description: (The reference letters refer to the Figure).

(1) The flat treadle (A) is moved up and down by a rhythmical movement of the foot.

(2) The deadman (C) is socketed at its lower end into an extension of the treadle and moves up and down with the treadle, but is free to move backwards and forwards as the up and down motion of the deadman causes the crank (F) to rotate.

(3) The driving wheel (B) is turned by the crank which is fastened to an extension of the axle on which the driving wheel rotates.

(4) A double driving band (described more fully in the section called 'Attaching the Driving Band') drives the two drive wheels (T and S) on the spinning head (*Figure 2.4*).

(5) The tension screw (E) is used for adjusting the tension on the driving band by moving the entire spinning head.

(6) The Mother of All (shown as G in *Figure 2.4*) carries the two uprights (the maidens 'D') between which the actual spinning is done.

(7) With reference to *Figure 2.4 A* the wool from the rolag is fed into the hollow spindle (X) and emerges on the other side of the leather bearing loop (Y1).

(8) Coming out of the spindle the wool passes over one of the hooks (V) on the flier (W).

(9) From the hook, the wool feeds down on to the bobbin (U).

(10) The bobbin drive wheel (T) causes the bobbin to rotate when driven by the driving band.

(11) The flier drive wheel (S) likewise causes the flier to rotate but, because the diameter of the bobbin drive is smaller than the flier drive, the bobbin turns faster than the flier.

22

The beauty of the action of the wheel can now be seen. Remembering that the whole point of spinning is to twist the wool from the rolag and for convenience wind it on the bobbin, one cannot help but admire the ingenuity of the unknown inventor who arranged that the wheel give the maximum amount of twist to the wool but still allowed for the bobbin to collect the thread slowly. This is automatically accomplished through the bobbin and the flier revolving at slightly different speeds, and without this innovation, the spinning wheel would be very much less efficient.

Attaching the Driving Band

The driving band transmits the motion of the driving wheel to both the bobbin and the flier and is normally made of a length of stout, strong, highly twisted twine. Italian twine, Mechrame twine, or similar high quality twine should be used, as the driving band is subject to wear. The operation of fitting the driving band to the spinning wheel is carried out as follows:

(1) Adjust the tension screw so as to move the spinning head to the limit of its travel in the direction of the driving wheel.

(2) Take the free end of the twine and follow the instructions given below exactly:

(i) Pass the end completely around the driving wheel, guiding it with one hand while maintaining it in place in the groove of the wheel with a steady tension from the other hand.

(ii) Thread the end around the bobbin drive wheel.

(iii) Return the end to the driving wheel but make certain that on the return the end passes over the previous lay of the twine. This crossing of the two sections of the drive band is important to keep the band tracking on the wheels. Neglect the crossover and the band will come off at the first few rotations.

(iv) Pass the end around the driving wheel the second time.

(v) Return the end to the spinning head and thread around the flier drive wheel.

(vi) Bring the end back to the driving wheel, lay the two free ends of the twine together after pulling all taut and oversew together to form a continuous smooth running band. Clip away the surplus ends. Tighten the tension screw to adjust the driving band to grip firmly. Poor quality twine will stretch with use and the join may have to be broken after short use and the band tightened in order to give further adjustment to the tension screw. High quality twine will avoid this annoyance.

Figure 2.4A

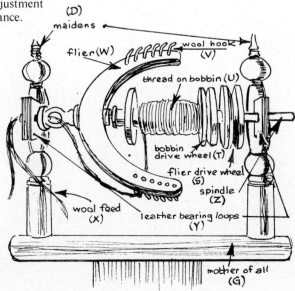

Spinning head of spinning wheel

25

The essence of good spinning is an even, non-jerky feed of wool into the spinning head. This cannot be accomplished unless movement of hands and feet are synchronized into a smooth, rhythmical flow of motion. Fortunately, the correct movements are completely natural and should become second nature after a little practice. Now let us look to the actual technique of spinning:

(1) Around the bobbin is tied a length of wool thread. (As with spindle spinning, a piece of machine wool will do for this).

(2) Carry this piece over a hook (any hook will do) on the flier and 'offer it up' at the hole at the inside end of the spindle eye. Refer *Figure 2.6*.

(3) Use a hooked length of wire (as shown in *Figure 2.5*) and hook the end of the wool out of the spindle eye.

(4) Tease the end of this pilot piece of thread.

(5) Sit in comfort alongside the wheel with a basket of rolags close to hand.

(6) In the left hand hold the teased end of the pilot thread and lay parallel the end of a rolag held between finger and thumb. Refer *Figure 2.6*.

(7) With the right hand give the wheel a spin so the flier turns to the right and pick up the motion with the treadle.

(8) Start the movement slowly and let the twist run to the left hand.

(9) With the right hand pull out a few inches of wool to the thickness required and relieve the pressure on the left hand. The twist will pick up and the thread will feed through the left hand and into the spinning head.

(10) Hold the twist with the left hand again. Draw out wool with the right hand and repeat the performance. A few 'do's and dont's' are called for at this stage.

(i) Do not let the twist run beyond the back hand and into the main part of the rolag. Such carelessness results in a terrible mess.

(ii) Do not try to drive the wheel fast. The natural speed of rotation is soon sensed and the highest quality thread comes at this speed.

(iii) When joining on a new rolag bring both sections to a point to prevent a lump from forming.

(iv) Do not let the wheel reverse.

(v) Aim for big sweeping motions in spreading the wool between hands, resulting in a more natural feed and a very much less tiring operation.

(vi) Do continue to try, even though the wool tangles, the thread breaks and it seems impossible to fall into a natural rhythm of movement. If you carry on, suddenly, and for no apparent reason, the wool peels off the rolag, the twist takes up, the flier feeds on to the bobbin and everything goes right.

(11) As one section of the bobbin builds up with finished thread, shift the feed to another hook.

(12) As the bobbin fills, remove it, place it on the 'Lazy Kate' (the bobbin rack) *Figure 2.7* and replace it with an empty bobbin.

(13) When Lazy Kate is full, skein the wool on the 'Niddy Noddy' as discussed in the last section but one in this chapter.

The names used for the various parts of the spinning wheel and the accessories used with it appear somewhat strange but they are in universal use wherever spinning is done in English speaking countries and it is as well to become familiar with their use whether or not one approves of the terminology.

Figure 2.5

thread hook

Figure 2.6

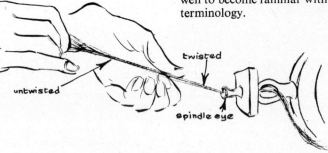

untwisted

twisted

spindle eye

Plying Thread

For many reasons a single thread is not satisfactory in all circumstances. It may be that the thread is too thin, not strong enough, is required to blend two grades of wool or two colours, etc. The answer in every case is to ply two or more threads together. This is done on the spinning wheel. To ply two or more threads, proceed as follows:

(1) On the Lazy Kate place as many full bobbins as there are to be plys in the finished thread.

(2) Thread on to an empty bobbin in the normal way but tie the ply threads to the pilot thread. Do not do this with one knot but spread the ties as shown in *Figure 2.8*.

(3) To regulate the tension of the twist, the left hand should both guide and control the ply threads into the spindle eye. The most usual error in plying is to make the plying too firm. Err on the loose side rather than the firm. Wool very seldom departs from its normal softness.

(4) To keep the ply threads in order as they feed, put them between the fingers. In more detail, lay the first thread over the first finger of the left hand, the second thread between the first and second fingers, the third ply thread between the second and third fingers and for four ply the last thread between the third and fourth fingers. In the rare event of more than four plys being needed, a cardboard guide with slots as shown in *Figure 2.9* can be used but first make sure your spindle eye will take the finished thickness of wool.

(5) Most importantly in plying, the machine must run counter to the normal direction. That is, if the usual direction of movement is observed, the individual threads will have been twisted with the driving wheel turning to the right. To ply in such a case the driving wheel must turn to the left or opposite to the previous direction.

Skein Winding

Thread wound on either the paper spills from spindle spinning or on the bobbins from wheel spinning, is not in a convenient form for handling further. Particularly for scouring, the thread should be in skeins. For the purpose of skeining thread, a Niddy Noddy as shown in *Figure 2.10* is most useful. The figure is self-explanatory, the wool being run off the Lazy Kate directly on to the Niddy Noddy. The only precaution to note is to tightly tie the skeins at at least four points by passing a tie round all the strands at that point and tying tightly. Only then should the moveable bars and axle be taken away to free the skein.

Scouring

There are possibly nearly as many different ways of washing the wool after spinning as there are spinners and who is to say which method is the best. However, there is no point in adopting harsh washing methods and scouring out all the natural oil in the home-spun. Certainly hot water should never be used to wash home-spun. At best, steeping in warm water will give sufficient aid to the self-cleaning characteristics of wool. At the worst, a short soak in a warm solution of the softest soap is all that is required, followed by several rinses in clear, slightly warm water.

In particular, think twice before using dye. There is a natural beauty to home-spun and enough shade variation in the colours of raw wool to allow for any reasonable pattern variation. Far better to introduce texture variety in knitting and weaving than to resort to the use of a lot of colour. However, as with so much else this is a matter of individual taste and must be left to the choice of the spinner or weaver.

And that brings to a close all that is thought necessary to say in regard to spinning. Sufficient to observe that those home crafters that gain proficiency in spinning will never lack a creative way in which to fill in their leisure and if inclined that way, they will always have a way of capitalising on their skill and time. Home-spun wool offered either for knitting or weaving will realise a very much higher price than can be obtained by shops for machine spun wool.

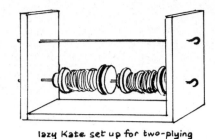

Figure 2.7

lazy Kate set up for two-plying

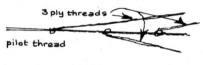

Figure 2.8

3 ply threads

pilot thread

knotting ply threads to pilot thread

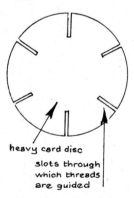

Figure 2.9

heavy card disc

slots through which threads are guided

plying guide

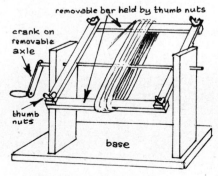

Figure 2.10

removable bar held by thumb nuts

crank on removable axle

thumb nuts

base

niddy-noddy or skein winder

CHAPTER THREE

Knitting with homespun

Hand knitting is too well known to the majority of crafters to be worth pursuing in detail here. There is, however, sufficient difference between homespun and machine spun wool to make some discussion of this subject of interest.

Characteristics of Wool

Under a microscope wool is seen to be a highly complex substance. The centre of the fibre is constructed of a series of canal-like cells. Around this central structure are further elongated cells and outside of these again is a layer of horny scales. The overall characteristics of wool as a fabric material is the great variation in cell types which make up a single wool fibre. Compared to other vegetable and animal fibres, wool is most complicated. Synthetic or man-made fabrics on the other hand are knitted or woven from very simple materials indeed.

However, from the point of view of hand-knitting, it is the outside of the wool fibre that is of the greatest immediate interest. As noted above, the outside of a wool fibre is covered with a series of cells forming over-laying scales. These scales have microscopic bracts almost like little hooks and the combination of these bracts and imbrications (the way in which the scales overlap, like tiles on a roof) means that one fibre of wool does not slide easily past another and will tend to hook, one with the other. This feature of wool explains why wool makes such warm clothing, why wool fabric is so strong and why wool is the most suitable fibre for hand-knitting.

Knitting Stitches

The method of interlocking threads in knitting is basically very different from the method used in weaving (discussed in the next chapter). Knitted fabrics are made from a series of interlocking loops as shown in *Figure 3.1*. The size of the loops and the distance between the thread is determined by the tension applied to the thread during the knitting process and the actual thickness of the thread being used, not forgetting of course the size of the needles. Woollen thread can stand considerable stress from pulling, however, the amount of pull is not unlimited and while the thread may not immediately break from too great a tension, the natural very high wear resistance of wool can be sadly reduced.

Therefore there are two opposing requirements in knitting:

(i) To fill the gaps between the loops by drawing the loops close together.
(ii) The contrary need to leave the threads as loose as possible without the knitting being so loose as to lose shape.

Knitting Wools

Most manufacturers of hand-knitting wools offer two classes of thread:

(1) The so-called 'Woollens' made in a very similar way to the homespun as described in the last chapter.

Figure 3.1

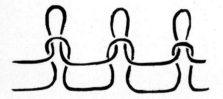

interlinking loops of a knitted fabric

(2) Worsted, which is treated in a very different way at certain stages. In the making of worsted thread an extra combing process is carried out after carding and this combing removes all broken wool and short pieces, rendering the wool much smoother. After combing, the wool is then stretched by a series of rollers with one roller in each pair travelling faster than the other so that the individual fibres are, after combing and rolling, lying in the same direction, each parallel with the others. After spinning this produces worsted thread; very strong, comparatively smooth thread. It is typical of a worsted cloth that each individual thread can be seen and any fluffiness has been shorn away in the manufacturing process.

Knitted Garments

Very few home-spinners can make true worsted thread, whereas most machine spun thread has at least, in part, the characteristics of worsted. From this it follows that, with few exceptions, homespun wool cannot be used for the complete range of knitted wear for which machine spun wool is suitable.

Worsted thread, if it is good quality, can be knitted much tighter than homespun and is well suited to form-fitting garments, while homespun must be reserved for looser-fitting outdoor and sporting jerseys and such like. Not that this is a disadvantage, for the fluffiness of homespun admirably fills in the gaps between the knitting loops and produces a fabric which, by trapping the air, is very much warmer to wear and definitely more wind-resistant than worsted.

Because homespun knitting produces a thicker fabric, homespun garments fit looser and are not subject to the same stretching effect during wearing, and this, in combination with the heavier weight of wool, gives them the longer wearing quality for which homespun is noted. Homespun thread adds to the distinctive character of homespun garments, being less even in thickness than machine spun thread, but this latter quality does complicate the process of knitting, especially if the thread has been spun very unevenly.

Hand-Knitting with Homespun

An experienced knitter will have no difficulty in making a success of using homespun but it must be remembered that:

(i) The pattern selected must be suitable for homespun.

(ii) The tension used should be much less than when machine spun thread is being knitted.

(iii) The needles used must be several times larger than for knitting with machine spun thread.

(iv) The number of stitches must be reduced in proportion to the increase in size of the needles used.

(v) Form-fitted garments should not be attempted.

(vi) Unless special machine spun hand-knitting wools are used, homespun will produce garments superior in almost every respect for outdoor use.

This is especially so if the wool has not been treated in such a way as to lose the natural oil in the wool.

The above statements are all generalisations and let us hasten to add (in order to forestall irate complaints from highly skilled crafters) that there are exceptions to every rule and none more so than in the field we have been discussing.

Machine Knitting

Home knitting machines are a very great aid to the speedy production of knitted garments. In general, difficulties can be expected in using homespun thread in these machines. The rather thick, fluffy, uneven thickness of homespun will make for trouble in easy feeding of the wool through the 'latch hooks' of the average knitting machine. The following hints may help to resolve these difficulties, although much depends on the quality and evenness of the homespun and on the characteristics of the particular machine being used:

(i) Use every other needle, or even every third needle on the needle bed when 'threading up' homespun on to the machine.
(ii) Use the lowest tension possible.
(iii) Use only the very simplest stitch patterns; certainly do not attempt patterns that require groups of needles to pull the homespun simultaneously.
(iv) Wax the thread before machine knitting. This is easily done by drawing the thread through a block of super-fine paraffin wax obtainable from a chemist or drug store.
(v) When joining the wool, tail each of the ends out into a long 'rat tail' to avoid as far as possible, a double thickness of wool in any latch needle.
(vi) Work slowly and steadily so that when the wool starts running, it continues without jerks and stops.

Knitting Unspun Wool

Skilled knitters can produce attractive garments by knitting directly from the fleece. This is done in the following way:

(i) A clean, long-staple fleece is selected and carefully sorted, discarding all uneven pieces, matted wool, horny wool and pieces with knots and burrs.
(ii) A lock of even wool is withdrawn and held in the palm of the hand with part of the wool protruding beyond the palm and below one knitting needle which is held between the finger and thumb of that hand.
(iii) The other hand is used to draw out a length of wool, in such a way that a fairly even thread is formed. This is knitted in with large needles using plain stitch and another length drawn out.
(iv) The needles are not laid down, some practice being necessary to ensure that the completed knitting is held on the needle while the raw wool is drawn out.
(v) The technique of handling needles and wool together becomes surprisingly easy and while it is not possible to knit as fast as with prepared thread, the process is not as slow as would appear from the above description and is certainly worth doing if fleece wool is available. The resulting garment tends to be very fluffy, very warm and hard-wearing.

Patterns for Homespun

It is possible to adapt many published patterns for the use of homespun and a keen knitter will have little difficulty in producing individual patterns. In adapting a pattern or working from one designed by oneself, it is necessary to try out the needle size, the thread thickness and the tension to ensure the correct number of stitches for a given width. To do this, knit a test square as follows:

Cast on about 20 stitches and knit 10 or 20 rows and use this as a check of the pattern against the measurements required.

The pattern can be varied by:

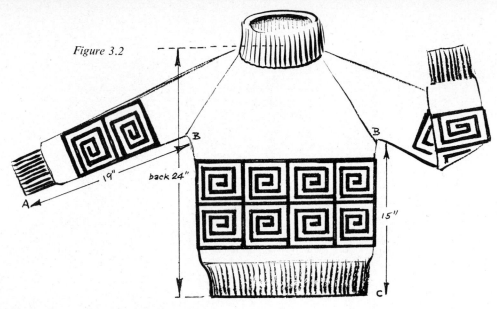

Figure 3.2

19"   back 24"   15"

ski sweater

detail of pattern for ski sweater

(i) Changing the number of stitches.
(ii) Using different size needles.
(iii) Altering the tension of working.
   Here are instructions for two useful and typical garments which are ideal for knitting in homespun wool.

Ski Sweater
Highly effective ski clothes can be knitted from homespun, of which the ski sweater shown in *Fig. 3.2*, with the pattern given below, is an excellent example.

Ski Sweater in Chunky Homespun

Abbreviations:		Measurements:	Requirements:
mc	Main Colour	Back 24″ to Roll Collar	1 lb Chunky Homespun
pc	Pattern Colour	Sleeve to Armhole 19″	Wool Main Colour
sts	Stitches	Side Seam 15″	8 oz Chunky Homespun
ss	Stocking Stitch		Wool Pattern Colour
rib	1 purl 1 plain		Pair No. 7 and No. 4
p	Purl		Knitting Needles
k	Plain		4 No. 10 Needles for
psso	Pass slip stitch over		Roll Collar
tog	Together		

Front
Using No. 7 Needles cast on 98 sts.
Knit into back of sts.
Then rib for 3 inches.
Change to No. 4 Needles and do six rows of ss in mc.

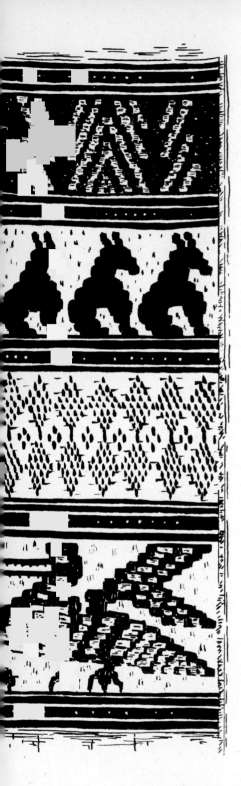

Commencing Pattern:

Row 1
    2 } ss in pc

3. (K. 2pc, 22mc) 4 times; then 2pc
4. (P. 2pc, 22mc) 4 times; then 2pc
5. K. 2pc, 2mc, 22pc, 2mc, 22pc, 2mc, 22pc, 2mc, 22pc
6. P. 22pc, 2mc, 22pc, 2mc, 22pc, 2mc, 22pc, 2mc, 2pc
7. K. (2pc, 2mc, 2pc, 18mc) 4 times; then 2pc
8. P. (2pc, 18mc, 2pc, 2mc) 4 times; then 2pc
9. K. (2pc, 2mc, 2pc, 2mc, 14pc, 2mc) 4 times; then 2pc
10. P. (2pc, 2mc, 14pc, 2mc) 4 times; then 2pc
11. K. (2pc, 2mc, 2pc, 2mc, 2pc, 10mc, 2pc, 2mc) 4 times; then 2pc
12. P. (2pc, 2mc, 2pc, 10mc, 2pc, 2mc, 2pc, 2mc) 4 times; then 2pc
13. K. (2pc, 2mc, 2pc, 2mc, 2pc, 2mc, 6pc, 2mc, 2pc, 2mc) 4 times; then 2pc
14. P. (2pc, 2mc, 2pc, 2mc, 6pc, 2mc, 2pc, 2mc, 2pc, 2mc) 4 times; then 2pc
15. K. (2pc, 2mc, 2pc, 2mc, 2pc, 6mc, 2pc, 2mc, 2pc, 2mc) 4 times; then 2pc
16. P. (2pc, 2mc, 2pc, 2mc, 2pc, 6mc, 2pc, 2mc, 2pc, 2mc) 4 times; then 2pc
17. K. (2pc, 2mc, 2pc, 2mc, 10pc, 2mc, 2pc, 2mc) 4 times; then 2pc
18. P. (2pc, 2mc, 2pc, 2mc, 10pc, 2mc, 2pc, 2mc) 4 times; then 2pc
19. K. (2pc, 2mc, 2pc, 14mc, 2pc, 2mc) 4 times; then 2pc
20. P. (2pc, 2mc, 2pc, 14mc, 2pc, 2mc) 4 times; then 2pc
21. K. (2pc, 2mc, 18pc, 2mc) 4 times; then 2pc
22. P. (2pc, 2mc, 18pc, 2mc) 4 times; then 2pc
23. K. (2pc, 22mc) 4 times; then 2pc
24. P. (2pc, 22mc) 4 times; then 2pc
25. K. pc
26. P. pc

These 26 rows comprise the main pattern and are repeated from Row 3 – 24sts to a pattern.

Now commence shaping armholes:

In main colour working in ss, K1, Slip 1, K1, psso.

Cast off one stitch at beginning and end of each knit row. So K1, Slip 1, psso, k to last 3 sts. K2 tog, K1. until 30 rows have been worked from armhole, then cast off ten sts in centre for neck.

Continue working shoulder, casting off one stitch at the beginning and end of each Knit row until all sts have been cast off.

So: K1, Slip 1, K1, psso to last two sts on neck edge, K2 tog.

Rejoin wool at the neck edge of the second shoulder and work as follows:

1st Row – K2 tog; k until 3sts remain, K2 tog; K1
2nd Row – Purl

Repeat until all sts have been cast off.

Back

Repeat as for the front but continue casting off until 22 sts remain. Put these on a spare needle.

Sleeves

Cast on 40 sts on No. 7 needles.

Knit into back of sts.

Rib for 2½ inches.

Add on 8 sts evenly over the last rib row by knitting into the front and back loops of the stitch.

Change to No. 4 needles and knit six rows in ss.

Then do two patterns for the front.

From then on knit in ss increasing one stitch at each end of every 6th row until 72 sts are on the needles.

32

Shape Armhole:
1st Row – K1, Slip 1, K1, psso; knit to last 3 sts; K2 tog, K1
2nd Row – Purl
Repeat until 11 sts remain; cast off.
Sew up sweater.

Neck
Using No. 10 Needles, pick up and knit 11 sts on left sleeve, 22 sts across
the back, 11 sts on right sleeve, 34 sts on the front.
Knit these 78 sts in rib for 7 inches. Cast off.

Balaclava Helmet
A Balaclava helmet as shown in *Figure 3.3* may not be glamorous but it is
unquestionably protective. Made in homespun, with the wool oil left in
it, it is as effective against loss of heat from the upper part of the body as
any garment can be. As can be seen from the figure and the pattern given
below, this particular design of helmet has a chest and shoulder protector
woven into the design to increase its effectiveness.

Pattern
Requirements:
4 oz Homespun
Pair No. 8 Needles

Back
With No. 8 needles cast on 70 sts.
Knit 74 rows in plain knitting.
Cast off 23 sts for shoulder; K 68.
Cast off 23 sts for shoulder; K 45. (Put these 45 sts on a spare needle).

Front
As for Back.
Now you have 90 sts on spare needles.
Take the centre front. Slip 23 sts on 2nd needle then:
Knit 22 sts in 2 Purl 2 Plain rib from centre front.
Knit 45 sts in 2 Purl 2 Plain rib across back, then:
Knit the 23 sts in 2 Purl 2 Plain rib left on needle.
Now work in rib on these 90 sts for 36 rows (Neck).
Still working in ribbing, cast off 4 sts at beginning of the next 8 rows (58
sts left).
Work these 58 sts for 24 more rows.
Cast on 16 sts at the beginning of the next 2 rows.
Knit 24 rows still in ribbing.
Next row K 2 tog. to end of row.
Next row K 2 tog. to end of row.
Pull rest of sts into a tight circle.
Sew up shoulders and centre front seams.

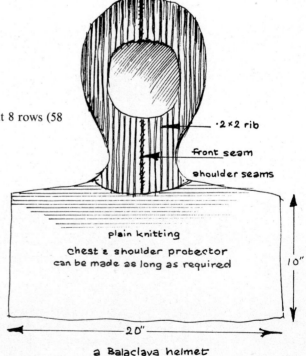

Figure 3.3

·2×2 rib

front seam

shoulder seams

plain knitting

chest & shoulder protector
can be made as long as required

10"

20"

a Balaclava helmet

CHAPTER FOUR

Looms and weaving

Weaving, one of the most ancient of crafts, is at the same time both simple and extremely elaborate. Let us explain this apparent contradiction in terms. Weaving in itself is simply the operation of darning, carried out in a frame called a loom. As in darning, a thread is carried under and over a number of other threads so that an interlocking pattern is formed. This is shown in *Figure 4.1*. By convention, the fixed threads (shown by the open lines in the figures) are called 'the warp' while the loose thread that passes backwards and forwards over and under the warp is called 'the weft', sometimes 'the woof'.

The simplest of looms is a frame as shown in *Figure 4.2*.

Primitive Loom
The warp is tied to a framework of sticks lashed together. The weft is threaded backwards and forwards. In such a loom the process of picking up each alternative warp thread in turn becomes laborious and the pulling through of a long weft thread behind a needle leads to tangles and endless trouble.

Heddles
The first difficulty is resolved by arranging for a device called a 'Heddle' to raise every second warp thread and form a clear passage between the alternative warp threads. This is shown in *Figure 4.3*. As can be seen, a simple heddle consists of a piece of string tied around every second warp thread and in turn tied to a stick. Raising the stick lifts every second thread and forms a tunnel called in loom language a 'shed'. Two such heddle 'tie ups' and thus the process of weaving is made considerably faster.

Shuttles
To overcome the difficulty of dragging a long length of weft behind a needle the weft should be wrapped around the needle and paid off as it passes through the shed. Such a needle becomes a shuttle and a number of different forms of shuttle are shown in *Figure 4.4*. Shuttles A, B and C in the figure are elementary shuttles on which the weft must be wound by hand. D and E carry a shuttle bobbin, the action of which can be seen from *Figure 4.5* and in addition shuttle E is fitted with two rollers so that it will run easily when thrown through a wide shed.

Beams
Even a comparatively narrow piece of cloth requires a large number of warp threads. The number of warp threads per inch of width are given in a term called 'a dent' of which more will be said later. Suffice to note here that a very coarse cloth will be woven at 5 dents per inch while a very fine one will run 30 dents to the inch. Hence a moderately fine piece of cloth woven, say, 15 dents to the inch and, say, being 20 inches wide will require 300 warp threads. To 'tie on' to a simple frame, 300

Figure 4.1

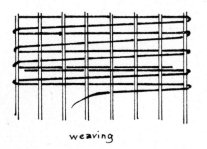

weaving

Figure 4.2

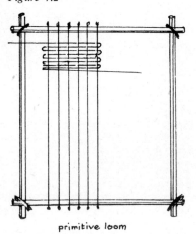

primitive loom

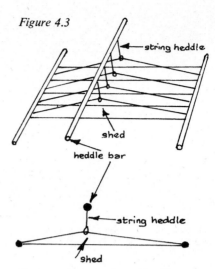

Figure 4.3

string heddle

shed

heddle bar

string heddle

shed

forming a shed by using a heddle

threads, to feed these through 300 heddles and to keep each thread at the same tension is a tiresome task if only 20 or so inches of cloth can be woven at each 'tie on'. With any loom the process of 'setting up' for weaving is a lengthy task.

The answer to the last problem is to fit the loom with beams. These are shown in *Figure 4.6*. As can be seen the beams are rollers, one carrying long lengths of warp, while the finished cloth is rolled on to the other. Each beam is fitted with a form of locking mechanism which allows the finished cloth to be rolled on to the cloth beam while additional warp is rolled off the warp beam. The warp can then be brought back to tension so that further weaving can proceed. The process of putting the warp on the loom is often referred to as 'Beaming On'.

Reeds

The weft thread when passed through the shed by the shuttle lies several inches away from its final position and has to be forced back into place. In the most primitive of looms this is done with a flat stick. An advance on using a stick is to use a comb and certain types of looms use this method today. However, by far the most usual way is to use a metal reed which is a series of metal strips or wires held in a frame. As supplied, reeds are sized by a number signifying the number of dents to the inch. Hence a No. 10 reed has ten spaces between the wires to every inch of length; No. 15, fifteen dents to each inch, and so on. The warp threads run through the spaces in the reed and the reed is swung so that it can follow down the line of the warp and drive the weft into place and at the same time space the warp. See *Figure 4.7*.

To recapitulate what has been said—the essentials of a loom are:

(1) *The Frame* – which carries the warp thread.
(2) *The Heddles* – which separate the warp threads to form a shed through which the shuttle is passed.
(3) *The Shuttle* – which carries the supply of weft and is used to lay this weft so it interlocks with the warp to form the web.
(4) *The Beams* – which allow of a greater length of web to be woven than can be held by the frame.
(5) *The Reed* – which both spaces the warp and beats the weft into place.

A Practical Loom

All the above parts of a loom must be so assembled that they can be brought into use, conveniently, quickly, and in the correct sequence. With two sets of heddles only the simplest patterns can be woven. These are known as 'Tabby' weaves where every warp thread is crossed over and under alternately by the weft thread. Certainly tabby weave is the most useful of all weaves. In fact, it can be regarded as the basic weave and very few looms are ever set up so that tabby weave cannot be done in addition to any other more elaborate weaving pattern that may be accomplished. Such fabrics as the common varieties of calicos, muslins, hopsack,

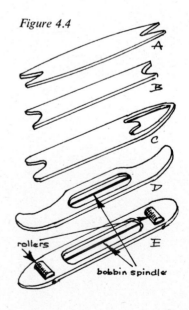

Figure 4.4

A

B

C

D

rollers

E

bobbin spindle

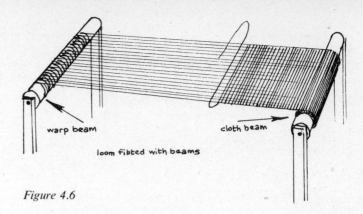

Figure 4.6

loom fitted with beams

warp beam

cloth beam

Figure 4.5

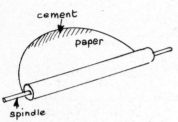

cement

paper

spindle

A. making the bobbin former

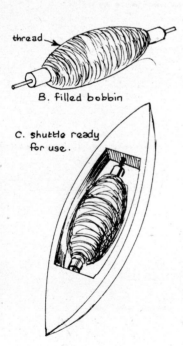

thread

B. filled bobbin

C. shuttle ready for use.

bobbin shuttle

tweeds and other fabrics, including a number of Scottish tartans, can be carried out in basic tabby weave.

However, many weavers find it too limiting, being unable to introduce the greater range of textural variety that they desire. It therefore follows that a very great number of loom types have been developed to allow essential loom components to be arranged in a way most convenient to handle more than two heddle sets and produce some particular style or styles of weaving more elaborate than tabby weave.

The next few chapters will therefore be devoted to a discussion on some of the more common types of looms, the way they should be operated and the classes of weaving which each of them will accomplish.

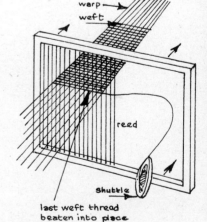

Figure 4.7

warp

weft

reed

shuttle

last weft thread beaten into place

batten (reed plus frame) being used to beat weft into place on the warp.

36

CHAPTER FIVE

Tapestry weaving

There are two meanings to the term 'tapestry weave', these are:

(1) A type of weave where openly-spaced warp threads are entirely hidden by the weft.

(2) A mural decoration, often in the form of wall panels, which is produced by using the weft to completely cover the warp. The techniques used in producing tapestry types of wall murals can be extended towards a type of weaving which is rapidly gaining recognition as possibly the ultimate in creative weaving. This new mode is of the greatest possible interest to advanced weavers seeking self-expression. Certainly it represents the greatest challenge to free design possible, as the combination of tapestry weaving techniques without the limitations imposed by traditional disciplines, results in work which is as free in form as any piece of modern art. But more of that later.

Tapestry Looms

The absolute simplicity of a tapestry loom is shown in *Figure 5.1*. The components of this loom are:

(1) A frame of any convenient size. It can be six feet or more in length and up to say five feet in width. A loom of this size will be stood on one end and worked vertically, using steps if necessary to reach the top. The timbers of such a frame need to be massive in construction and bolted together.

(2) Two beams which are part of the frame. One, the warp beam, is bolted solid as part of the frame, but the other, the tension beam, is fitted with an adjustable lock screw which when loosened will allow the beam to move along the slots in the frame to apply tension to the warp. Final adjustment of tension is given to the warp threads by lifting any individual threads that need tightening on to the warp tension stick, as shown in the figure alongside the tension beam.

(3) A number of shuttles are needed, one for each colour in the pattern. Only elementary shuttles are needed as shown in *Figure 5.2*.

(4) There is a group of parts for making the shed as shown in detail in *Figure 5.3* and used as follows:

(i) The shed stick, requiring to be of sufficient length to cross the width of the frame, is some 3 inches in width and about $\frac{1}{2}$ an inch in thickness, or perhaps, if of hard tough wood, a trifle thinner. This shed stick is threaded through alternate warp threads and the shed one way is made by turning the stick onto its edge. This raises half the threads to form the shed through which the shuttle passes.

(ii) The leash stick is harnessed as in the detail in *Figure 5.3(A)* and the warp threads which pass under the shed stick are threaded through the warp loops.

(iii) Two leash stick brackets are used. The brackets are made to the dimensions given in the detail in *Figure 5.3(B)*. To form the second shed, the shed stick lies flat and the leash stick is lifted on to the brackets as shown in *Figure 5.3*.

Figure 5.1

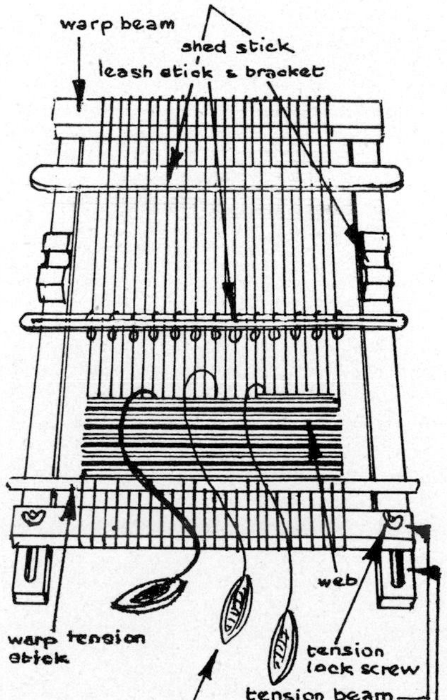

warp beam
shed stick
leash stick & bracket

web

warp tension stick
weft shuttles
tapestry loom
tension lock screw
tension beam
tension slots

Figure 5.3

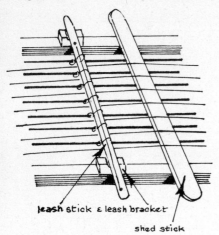

leash stick & leash bracket

shed stick

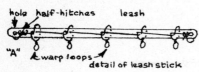

hole half-hitches   leash

"A"   warp loops

detail of leash stick

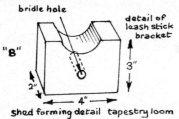

bridle hole

"B"

detail of
leash stick
bracket

3"

2"

4"

shed forming detail tapestry loom

Figure 5.4

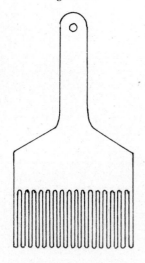

commercial tapestry beater

Figure 5.2

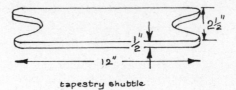

tapestry shuttle

(5) A beater is required to ensure that the weft is well driven home. A commercial type tapestry beater is shown in *Figure 5.4* while the home-made equivalent is depicted in *Figure 5.5*.

(6) The way in which tapestry weaving is carried out, and in particular the way the weft is beaten in sections, makes it difficult to prevent the edges (the selvedge) from coming together. Becoming waisted is the way tapestry weavers describe this fault as shown in *Figure 5.6*. A tenter-hook as in *Figure 5.7* can be used and is recommended for the prevention of waisting. The tenterhook shown in the figure is adjustable to suit any width of tapestry and should not prove difficult to make at home.

That concludes a review of the equipment required to enable fabric weaving to be undertaken. The actual weaving technique is discussed below, but it is worthy of note that for the outlay of a very few dollars, the expenditure of a little time and the use of a very basic tool kit will allow anybody – man, woman, or intelligent child – to provide themselves with a highly efficient loom for making a very wide range of materials. What better way to start into the wonderful field of weaving.

Tapestry Techniques

In general, tapestry weaving is used for the making of exceptionally strong firm material. Rugs, blankets, carpets, stool tops, upholstery cloth, drape material and fabrics for heavy outdoor wear are particularly suited to tapestry weaving methods. Strong patterns are a feature but it does not necessarily follow that tapestry woven cloth must be heavily patterned. Certainly the most intricate of designs can be carried out in tapestry weaving and these will be discussed in the next chapter.

The warp does not show; this is a feature of tapestry weaving and from this it follows that the strongest of warp thread should be used. Any twine type extra-strong fibre can be used. Italian twine, Mecrame twine, linen and cotton extra-strength floss and the like can be used. A really strong warp thread is well worthwhile, although no more essential in tapestry work than in any other weaving. The real point to the extra strength being that as the warp does not show, strength need not be sacrificed for looks.

A thick, rather fluffy, weft is an advantage as this type of thread will pack in well and cover the warp. Evenness in the thickness of the thread is not important in most applications and home-spun wool is particularly suited to tapestry. This is fortunate in one way, for a beginner at spinning is liable to have some quantities of rather uneven wool to hand and if this coincides with a beginning at weaving, with the choice being made of starting on tapestry work, then the combination is a very happy one.

Tapestry Patterns

Tapestry lends itself very well to the weaving of geometrical patterns. The Navaho Indians have a world-wide reputation for the production of striking saddle cloths and blankets woven in an identical manner to the craft artists of Sweden who have long exploited traditional tapestry methods.

40

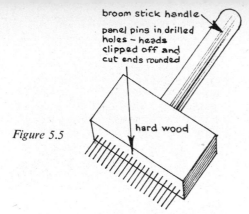

broom stick handle

panel pins in drilled holes – heads clipped off and cut ends rounded

hard wood

Figure 5.5

home made tapestry beater

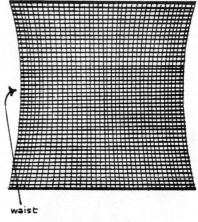

Figure 5.6

waist

waisting in weaving

Many cultures have produced art forms which are admirably suited to geometrical tapestry patterns and an example of such a pattern is shown in *Figure 5.8* and used as the basis of the discussion later in this chapter on tapestry weaving methods.

Almost all weavers develop their own style of laying out patterns in a way that will allow the reproduction of that pattern as a product of their particular loom. One of the more confusing aspects of instructional guides to weaving is the many varied methods advocated to lay out patterns. It seems that every second author has a different way to do this and so-called universal patterns are unnecessarily complicated to understand. The real answer seems to be a logical understanding of what is needed to produce a fabric of a given pattern, for example tapestry weaving.

'Setting Up' for Tapestry Weaving

To weave the Roimata Taroa pattern into a rug on a tapestry loom let us take it step by step as if an actual loom is being used. If this is an actual fact, so much the better:

(1) The size of the rug must first be decided and let us assume it to be standard size of 4 feet 6 inches length to 3 feet width.
(2) To allow plenty of freedom of movement within the loom, a frame 6 feet by 4 feet is ideal.
(3) The warp threads need to be 6 per inch, a good standard number of warps for tapestry weaving in general, and the beater can be made to suit this. The leash stick will need to be rigged 3 warp loops to the inch. Any need for a change in this standard warp separation for special jobs will require a new beater and the leash stick to be rigged to suit the new layout.
(4) For a three foot width of warp 219 warp threads are needed. The necessary number of threads is worked out thus:

At 6 per inch and 36 inches of width

$$6 \times 36 = 216$$

But this 216 represents the number of spaces so one extra thread is needed at the far end so the calculation becomes:

$$6 \times 36 = 216 + 1 = 217$$

The edges of the rug will be a weak point and it is wise to reinforce the edges or selvedges as they are called, by an extra thread at each end and this increases the number by 2, so the final calculation is:

$$6 \times 36 = 216 + 1 = 217 + 2 = 219$$

In case this calculation appears to have been worked out too laboriously it is well to remember how easy it is to make a mistake and as the warp will be used to calculate the pattern it is as well to calculate painfully in order to avoid the even more painful operation of pulling out all the weft threads because the pattern will not fit the warp as laid on the loom.
(5) The warp is now ready to be strung on the frame. Tying 219 separate strings around each beam is a tedious operation and this can be greatly simplified by adopting the method shown in *Figures 5.9* and *5.10*. The construction and rigging of the bridle stick is fairly clear from the two diagrams. The following points can be noted:

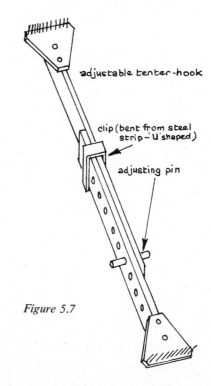

adjustable tenter-hook

clip (bent from steel strip – U shaped)

adjusting pin

Figure 5.7

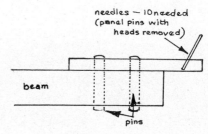

needles – 10 needed (panel pins with heads removed)

beam

pins

detail of tenter hook head

Figure 5.8

N.Z Maori design "Roimata Taroa"
(albatross tears)
– top left hand corner of pattern.

in natural wool colours, white, black
and fawn (shaded)

This design, adapted for weaving by
Roslyn Woollen Mills,
Dunedin, New Zealand is based on a
traditional Maori song where
"albatross tears" are symbolic of
something rare and beautiful.

Figure 5.9

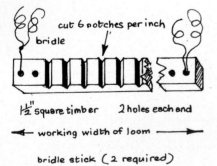

cut 6 notches per inch
bridle

1½" square timber   2 holes each end

← working width of loom →

bridle stick (2 required)

(i) The stick hangs in the bridle below the nails driven into the beam to carry the pull of the warp threads.

(ii) The cumulative pull, owing to the addition of the tension from each warp thread, can in wide weaving, prove to be very considerable indeed. Therefore, substantial size nails are needed to hold the bridle stick and these need to be driven well home and in a dead straight line. The warp position notches on the stick should not be cut deep enough as to weaken the stick.

(iii) The warp threads should be tied off at a bridle stick, say every two inches. Unless this is done, the breaking of a single warp thread will result in the slackening of all the warp. If this precaution is taken the warp can be rigged on to the loom simply by wrapping it alternately around each bridle stick in turn. The use of bridle sticks also greatly simplifies the spacing of the warp and the adjustment of tension.

(6) To support the selvedges the outside warp threads are doubled, running two together.

(7) The shed stick is next inserted through the warp picking up every second warp thread.

(8) The leash stick is next laid across the warp and the leashing rigged so as to pick up every thread which runs under the shed stick. Looking at the loom from the tension beam end, the leash stick is beyond the shed stick.

At this point, check carefully to be absolutely sure the warp threads are alternatively:

Under the shed stick, picked up in the warp loop.

Over the shed stick, free of the leash stick.

(9) The leash stick brackets are now tied one on each of the side frames about 12 to 18 inches above the tension beam.

(10) Each shuttle is filled with its individual weft colour. An extra shuttle can carry some spare warp thread for a purpose that is explained later.

The loom is now all set to start weaving, but before this can be done the pattern must be calculated.

Laying out the Pattern

The pattern must now be translated into terms which mean something in respect to the loom. The basic unit on the loom will be the distance between warp threads. In the usual spacing for tapestry weaving this will be one sixth of an inch or six spaces to one inch. Remember that it is six spaces between threads that equals one inch and not six threads, which only equal five sixths of an inch. With this basic measurement in mind the pattern can be critically examined, somewhat along these lines:

(1) Examine the pattern in *Figure 5.8*. Note the relationship which exists between the width of the various blocks of colour. These can be considered as being for a 3 foot wide rug:

(i) Fawn – 3 inches
(ii) Black – 3 inches
(iii) White – 5 inches overlapping the black 1 inch at each end.

(2) The above figures can be translated into terms of warp threads in this way. Always working from the left-hand side of the loom and the pattern:
(i) The edge of the first fawn row and hence the line of division between fawn and black will be warp thread number $3 \times 6 + 1 = 19$, if the selvedge thread is counted as one. The next division will be $13 + 3 \times 6 = 37$, the next 55, and so on adding 18 threads for each change. A piece of fawn weft thread can be lightly knotted around each of these threads to identify where the change in colour will take place when weaving.
(ii) Using the same reasoning for determining the change to white, when the white blocks are to be woven in, gives the first white change $1 \times 6 + 1 = 7$. This, for the end of the part white block at the beginning of the second row. For the beginning of the first complete white block in the second

row, the thread where the change takes place will be $7 + 1 \times 6 = 13$th thread. The end of this block in the second row will be $13 + 5 \times 6 = 43$rd thread, the next change $43 + 1 \times 6 = 49$th for the next change (being the beginning of the next block) is one inch further across.

All these calculations can, if necessary, be written down on paper somewhat in the way shown below:

Fawn/Black Change 19, 37, 55, 73, 91, 109, 127, 145, 163, 181, 199, 217 which last figure is, of course, the last warp thread and the double selvedge thread.

First Row White 25, 31, 61, 67, 97, 103, 133, 139, 169, 175, 205, 211, which leaves one inch of white block to finish at 217.

Second Row White 7, 13, 43, 49, 79, 85, 115, 121, 151, 157, 187, 193, which leaves four inches of white block to finish at 217.

The above table represents a pattern for the weft changes as translated into warp thread numbers. All the warp threads can then be identified by tying knots of weft thread of the correct colour to the appropriate thread.

The pattern can also show the lengthwise changes in pattern in the following way after noting the relationship which exists between the widths and the lengths of the pattern.

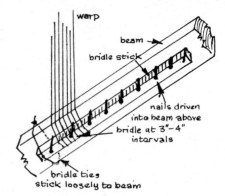

Figure 5.10

rigging bridle stick

Start
2 inches
Fawn/Black Change 19, 37, 55, 73 and so on in actual pattern draft.
3 inches
First Row White 25, 31, 61, 67, 97 and so on.
4 inches
Second Row White 7, 13, 43, 49, 79, 85 and so on.
3 inches
Fawn/Black Change as above.
Repeat

Any pattern in which the warp threads remain parallel can be drafted in this way. It may be mentioned that it is a highly special pattern that requires the warp to be other than parallel.

Individual weavers can no doubt produce their own particular way of modifying the method of pattern drafting given above. The actual layout of complicated patterns can be simplified for a given loom by numbering the position of groups of threads across the beams and putting the distances down the side frames. A ball-point pen can be used to put a mark on the wood work.

With all the preliminaries established, actual weaving can begin.

Tapestry Weaving
To emphasise what has been said before:

(1) The weft thread must be well 'beaten in' to form a firm web. Commence beating at the side opposite to where the shuttle has been removed. This allows the selvedge to be firmed and allows extra weft to be removed from the shuttle, so preventing waisting.

(2) The tenter-hook should be used immediately behind the 'weaving front'. The closer the tenter-hook is kept to the weaving, the straighter the edges will remain.

(3) The warp threads must be evenly tensioned. Use the tension stick to tighten any threads that go loose during weaving.

If these points are kept in mind right from the start, the finished product is sure to be successful.

The weaving itself can commence so:

To establish a firm edge four edges of warp thread are woven in before the pattern itself is begun.

(1) Raise the shed stick on edge and pass the shuttle through the shed so formed. A little practice is necessary to perfect the throwing of a shuttle and the movement is something akin to a flick of the wrist after sufficient weft has been removed from the shuttle so as not to snag it part-way across. A tapestry shuttle is not the easiest to throw and anybody who has gained proficiency with a tapestry shuttle of the type illustrated in *Figure 5.2* will have no difficulty with the torpedo type shuttles used on more conventional looms.

(2) Pay great care to the lay of the first lay of twine. See that it lies straight and firm and is beaten as far in as possible.

(3) Lower the warp stick and lift the leash stick on to its brackets and return the shuttle to lay in the second row of twine.

(4) Weave in two further rows of twine; beat well in. Leave 6 or 8 inches of twine beyond the selvedge and cut the first shuttle loose.

(5) The beginning and end of each thread is woven into the pattern as shown in *Figure 5.11*.

(6) When a shuttle runs out of thread, pick up in mid-weave as shown in *Figure 5.12*.

Study both *Figures 5.11* and *5.12* well. The techniques shown there are important to the finished appearance of the weaving. Do not neglect to beat the weft well home, particularly where a join has to be made.

(7) The pattern weaving begins. Note the interlocking which takes place at the edges of the pattern. The reason for a large number of shuttles now

Figure 5.11

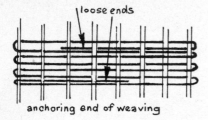
anchoring end of weaving

Figure 5.12

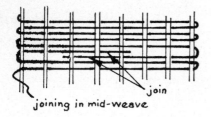
joining in mid-weave

Figure 5.13

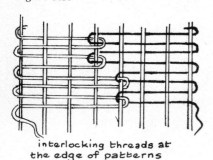
interlocking threads at the edge of patterns

becomes apparent. Fortunately each shuttle does not carry a great deal of weft and heavy cardboard is adequate for the construction. The shuttles have to be brought up through the warp threads and this means that the actual weaving must take place some distance from the weaving front where the weft is beaten in. Be sure to beat each row of weft in as it is finished. Do not yield to the temptation of doing several rows and then beating.

(8) Keep a careful watch on the distances down the loom so that pattern changes take place at the right place.

(9) When the correct length of web has been woven, the end is finished with the black weft, and then the four rows of twine.

(10) To finish the rug or any other article made in the above way, the warp threads are cut free six inches from the end of the weaving and, with a heavy needle, worked back into the four rows of twine until all are plaited in when the extra length may be trimmed off.

The completed rug, if carefully worked, will be an article worthy of considerable pride. The design in *Figure 5.8* is not a simple one to carry out, largely because of the number of changes of shuttle required with every row of weft. It is a very spectacular design and those who wish to make a first attempt at tapestry weaving may wish to settle for something a little more simple. It should be obvious that the design discussed can be made easier to weave if the pattern is made larger. If the fawn and black rows are six inches in width for instance, the number of shuttle changes are considerably reduced.

Figure 5.14

Pattern Development

Tapestry patterns can be developed from any picture, photograph or sketch. Consider the sketch in *Figure 5.14* which is a design for a floor mat. Examine the sketch point by point in this way.

(1) The overall length of the finished mat is to be 4 feet. Hence all measurements must be multiplied by four.

(2) The width will be $8 \times 4 = 32$ inches.

(3) The number of warp threads will be $32 \times 6 + 1 + 2 = 195$ (remembering one extra warp thread than spaces, 2 extra for the two double selvedges and 6 warp threads per inch).

(4) There are no changes of thread in the weft so only four shuttles will be needed. The pattern can now be written down.

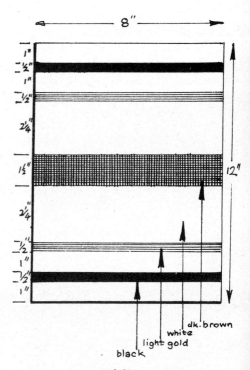

Sketch of floor mat

Start

White	1×4	$= 4$ inches – 193	the double selvedges count as one warp thread.
Black	$\frac{1}{2} \times 4$	$= 2$ inches – 193	
White	1×4	$= 4$ inches – 193	
Light Gold	$\frac{1}{2} \times 4$	$= 2$ inches – 193	
White	$2\frac{1}{4} \times 4$	$= 9$ inches – 193	
Brown	$1\frac{1}{2} \times 4$	$= 6$ inches – 193	
White	$2\frac{1}{4} \times 4$	$= 9$ inches – 193	
Light Gold	$\frac{1}{2} \times 4$	$= 2$ inches – 193	
White	1×4	$= 4$ inches – 193	
Black	$\frac{1}{2} \times 4$	$= 2$ inches – 193	
White	1×4	$= 4$ inches – 193	

Consider next a very much more complicated pattern to be developed directly from a photograph as in *Figure 5.15*. For the sake of simplicity here, details of the features are not developed in the pattern draft although they might well be. However, it is suggested where complicated minor features are required these be embroidered onto the finished pattern. The steps in developing the draft are as follows:

(1) Parallel lines are drawn as shown in the figure from every point where a pattern change is needed. The distance between these lines is then measured.

(2) The multiplying factor is next calculated. Let us say for example that the mural is to be 30 inches long. The overall length of the photograph is

Figure 5.15

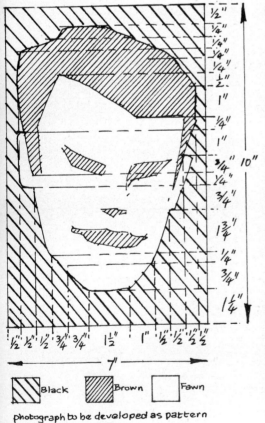

photograph to be developed as pattern draft

Black ⟋⟋⟋ Brown ⫽⫽ Fawn □

10 inches, hence every measurement must be multiplied by 3 in developing the draft. This figure 3 is the multiplying factor.

(3) The warp threads are next calculated: $7 \times 3 \times 6 + 1 + 2 = 129$.

(4) The warp thread numbers at which the pattern changes occur are next calculated and listed. These are worked out by reference to the photographic measurements, the multiplying factor and the number of warp threads per inch. So:

First Change $\frac{1}{2} \times 3 \times 6 + 1 = $ 10th warp thread
Second Change $10 + \frac{1}{2} \times 3 \times 6 = $ 19th warp thread
Third Change $19 + \frac{1}{2} \times 3 \times 6 = $ 28th warp thread
Fourth Change $28 + \frac{3}{4} \times 3 \times 6 = 41\frac{1}{2}$ say 42nd warp thread

And so on. The warp thread change points then become 10, 19, 28, 42, 55, 64, 73, 82, 127 and are for convenience written on to the photograph as in the figure. That should check with the number of warp threads, remembering that the first and last threads are double but allowed as a single thread in the calculation. A compromise is necessary where curved lines, as across the top of the head and down the line of the face are needed. Obviously these lines continuously cross the warp but it would be too complicated altogether to allow for this in the pattern. Hence it is assumed in the pattern that the changes take place in steps but when the actual weaving is being done a gradual movement across the warp is allowed. As a reminder that this is necessary a plus ($+$) or a minus ($-$) sign is added to the warp thread number where such a gradual change must take place. With reference to the photograph the pattern is now written down.

Start

Black $\frac{1}{2} \times 3 = 1\frac{1}{2}$ inches —127
Black $\frac{1}{4} \times 3 = \frac{3}{4}$ inch $= 40^+ \rightarrow$ Brown 40^+ to $55^- \rightarrow$ Black to 127
Black $\frac{1}{4} \times 3 = \frac{3}{4}$ inch $= 28^+ \rightarrow$ Brown 28^+ to $64^- \rightarrow$ Black to 127
Black $\frac{1}{4} \times 3 = \frac{3}{4}$ inch $= 19^+ \rightarrow$ Brown 19^+ to $82^- \rightarrow$ Black to 127

and the above operation is continued for the full length of the mural and the warp threads marked for change by putting markers on the appropriate thread. With a complicated pattern such as the above, there is need to watch the development in comparison to the photograph but surprisingly accurate developments can be made of figures, animals, landscapes, free form and other irregular forms by using the above method.

Some advanced tapestry techniques are discussed in the next chapter but before this chapter is completed it may be worthwhile to discuss a method of rug making which should appeal to a large number of people. This is discussed now:

Fleece Weaving

Highly satisfactory floor coverings, car and furniture covers and even bed covers can be made by the tapestry weaving technique, using raw wool directly from the fleece. The method by which such material is produced is extremely simple. The ideal wool needs to be of long staple. If obtainable one of the Leicester breeds or a Lincoln fleece will be most suitable but any reasonable long staple wool will do. The way the weaving is carried out follows:

(1) Rig the loom and carry out all operations up to the point where four rows of twine have been woven in – this is to the end of Instruction 5 of tapestry weaving earlier in this chapter.

(2) Tease the fleece wool out of the fleece, breaking it into tufts a little less than the thickness of a lead pencil.

(3) Slightly taper both ends of each tuft by pulling gently and lay the tufts, overlapping the tapered ends, across the shed.

(4) Start laying a little in from the edges, and, before commencing beating, finish each edge by placing a tuft half-way into the shed. The whole operation of making the edge is shown in *Figure 5.16*.

(5) Beat the loose wool well in. Do not worry about loose ends but note any patches which appear to be thin and add extra wool at this point.

46

Beat the added wool in. The success or failure of the operation is determined by the thoroughness with which the wool is consolidated during the beating.

(6) Change the shed and put in a second run of wool.

(7) Bring the end of the projecting tuft of wool from the last shed over the outside double warp thread. Pull this tuft tight and lay another half tuft (ready for edging with the next change of shed) on top and beat into place.

(8) Continue to weave in this fashion until at the end weave in the finishing four rows of twine and then plait in the warp ends.

The result will be an exceedingly comfortable article, firm, attractive and very warm.

The warp should be extra-strong as heavy beating is required.

No definite design can be worked in but by using different shades of natural wools an excellent appearance can be achieved.

It should be pointed out that this process of weaving does not take a great deal of time. Fleece wool is not expensive as compared to other quality weaving materials, the cost of making a suitable loom for oneself is very moderate and one can have a complete floor covering, set of upholstery or car covers at but a fraction of what articles of comparable quality would cost.

Tapestry weaving introduces do-it-yourself techniques that allow the ordinary person to achieve considerable satisfaction by showing them how their skill and patience can produce articles that will be the envy of all those who see them.

Figure 5.16

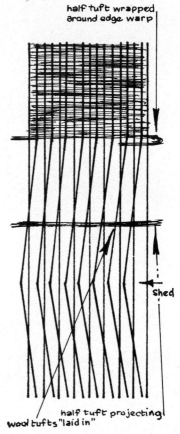

half tuft wrapped around edge warp

shed

half tuft projecting

wool tufts "laid in"

fleece weaving

Modern techniques

The final section in the last chapter advanced the very simple technique of producing high quality, low cost, floor and upholstery covers. This chapter completes the possibility of supplying all the soft furnishings of a modern home by giving details of the making of ultra-modern hangings and murals for window drapes, wall decoration and room dividers.

A charge is oft-times laid against the craft of weaving, accusing conservatism, traditionalism and a wholly mechanistic approach towards the artistic content of woven products. Whatever truth there may have been in such a charge in the past, modern designer craftsmen have introduced as much free expression into their work as in any of the more recognised disciplines of modern art.

Modern art weaving stresses texture and form, with colour in general, a secondary consideration. In comparison to earlier weavers, today's advanced weaver uses the broad sweep of his final creation to portray the simplicity of large textured masses and balance of form. An acceptable art form must be suited to a particular context which the artist has anticipated and allowed for in his design. A wall panel to be successful must become a part of a specific atmosphere, a furniture fabric must be complementary to the surroundings, a dress fabric suit the occasion.

Textural Weaving

Textures produce a play of light and shade on a surface. Weaving lends itself beautifully to textural display. Not that this mode of highlighting features, by changes of texture, is new in the field of fabric pattern design, but the modern trend is to play down other methods in favour of surface changes.

Texture design implies the handling of large areas and integrating the parts to form a whole. It is the opposite of the fussiness of Victorianism and requires breadth of outlook. This aspect of seeing the whole as one piece is the reason why it is suggested that textural designs be carried out within the large frame of a tapestry loom rather than on the more limited scope of a conventional loom.

The first point of departure from the usual methods of weaving comes in the choice of materials used in textural weaving. Virtually anything that can be held in place by a warp or a combination of warp and weft is fair choice for the adventurous.

In *Figure 6.1* the combination of two widths of cane, the piping cord (a heavy soft cotton cord) used for the warp, together with the gap between the cane weft where the piping cord keeps them apart, makes an interesting study in light and shade and one which changes as the light values and direction shift with the sun's movement. Such combinations have infinite possibilities and can be most useful for indoor and outdoor shades and dividers. The making of such an article (it hardly seems appropriate to call it a fabric) is very simple. The screen shown in the figure is made as follows on a simple tapestry to a suitable length and width as described in Chapter 5.

Figure 6.1

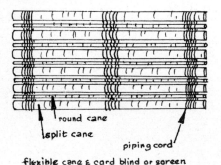

round cane

split cane

piping cord

flexible cane & cord blind or screen

(1) Calculate the position of the warp cords and set up double warp threads (that is a double length of piping cord) in lots of five to the number required. There are three sets of five doubled cords in the figure but a greater number may be more appropriate in a different situation. Unless the width is narrow it is not recommended that less than 3 sets of warp threads be used for an article of this sort.

(2) Put the shed stick in place and re-rig the leash to suit the warp and in such a fashion that the single warp of the double warp threads will be in different sheds.

(3) Select the cane free from blemishes (cut to length), seal with a good quality wood sealer, sand the surface lightly and finish with enamel or varnish.

(4) Open the first shed with the shed stick and insert the first length of split cane, forcing it well back into the warp.

(5) Lower the shed stick and raise the leash stick. Position the warp threads so the pairs are together with one thread passing over and the other one of the pair passing under the cane.

(6) Place a length of round cane in position and check that the two cane pieces in position are exactly at right angles to the warp. This is important for the final appearance and must be carefully checked and adjusted until it is sure that at each insertion the screen continues to be made completely square.

(7) Continue until the screen has reached the correct length.

(8) Release the double warp threads, one at a time, and bind the twin warps together at the rear of the first slot. This is shown in *Figure 6.2*. Use strong thread – bootmakers' thread will do – of a matching colour to the warp. Lock the threads with a coat of clear cement.

(9) The screen can be mounted as and where it is most suited to the decor of the home. A room divider of this type can be highly effective in contemporary furnishing schemes.

Figure 6.2

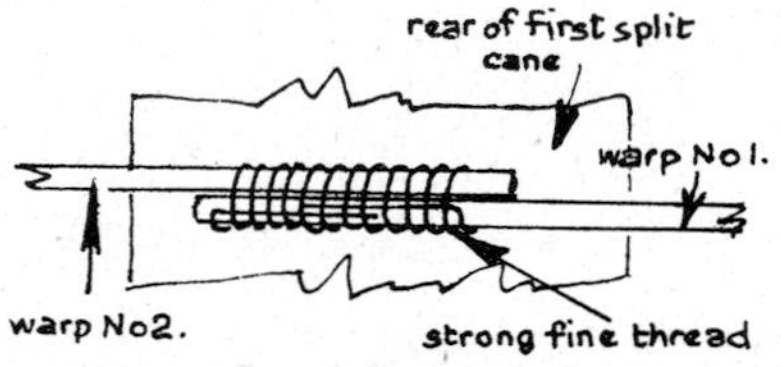

whipping the two ends of warp pairs together

Figure 6.3 shows a useful variation of the screen shown in *Figure 6.1*. In the pattern shown, strips of leather are used to increase the textural contrast both horizontally and vertically, and vertically split cane rods have been used to make the screen much more rigid and hence less subject to banging around in a breeze or draft.

Using the general methods of tapestry weaving makes the production of screens of this type an exceedingly simple task and all sorts of materials can be conveniently incorporated into the design. Woollen warp threads in homespun are not really strong enough but wool does make highly desirable warp threads if plied with a reinforcing ply of high strength twine or linen cord. To do this:

(1) Set up the Lazy Susan (refer Chapter 2) with three or four bobbins of lightly spun wool and one bobbin of strong twine or cord.

(2) Set the spinning wheel to ply, and, keeping a firm tension on the cord ply, spin the woollen threads around the cord centre. If the wool is allowed to feed more freely than the cord the cord will be completely hidden by the woollen cover.

Plying reinforcing into woollen threads permits the use of the textural qualities of wool to be used in the warp threads of screens where high strength in the warp is of considerable importance.

In the production of screens the weaving of several rows of fabric thread into the design should not be overlooked. As said earlier, screens of the type under discussion owe much of their appeal to the textural qualities and the contrast effected by changes in texture and any means of enhancing these features should not be overlooked.

Figure 6.3

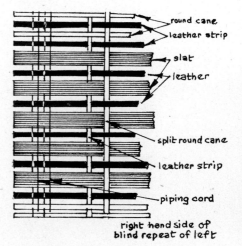

rigid cane, cord and leather blind or screen

Free Weft Weaving

As long as the convention is held that the weft thread must travel at right angles across the warp, the possibilities of free design are limited. However, let the weft travel in any direction, requiring only that it be locked into the warp enough times for it to become part of the web and

Figure 6.4

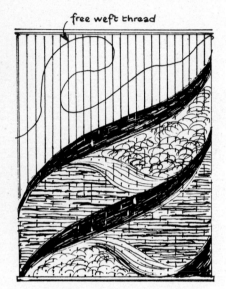

free weft thread

free weft weaving

the situation becomes entirely different. *Figure 6.4* gives an indication of the possibilities of this freedom. In conventional tapestry weaving, the weft changes at every point (in a horizontal plane) where there is a colour or textural change required by the pattern. In free weft weaving the weft follows the line of the pattern and does so irrespective of direction with the exception of vertical and even here some ingenuity will often allow a solution to the problem.

In general the weft is first used to lay in the outline of the particular area being dealt with and then the centre is woven in. Small areas which are too small to fill in with the normal shuttle are manipulated by miniature shuttles and even darning needles. Free weft patterns vary to the full limit of the imagination and ingenuity of the crafter. In many respects free weft weaving can be likened to painting where the design emerges as the work proceeds. Free warp weaving can readily be undertaken on a conventional loom but of course the normal reed cannot be used. In fact, in many cases with this style of weaving, a single metal rod is the only practical way of beating the weft home and is a necessary part of the loom equipment.

Ideally suited to the production of pieces in the contemporary style, free weft weaving is a challenge to all who may feel that they can produce more highly creative work if freed from the limitations imposed by conventional methods of weaving.

Diagonal Warp Weaving

A minor departure from conventional weaving styles can be given by setting up a tapestry loom with the warp threads running diagonally as shown in *Figure 6.5*. By so doing many unusual shapes, especially geometrical figures, can be woven in at angles requiring much more intricate work than if the loom were threaded up in the usual way. As with all unconventional methods of weaving, including the free weft method, particular attention must be paid to the selvedge and in the diagonal warp method extra warp threads running the length of the loom as in the normal way must be used for the sole purpose of providing a firm edge.

Free Warp, Free Weft Weaving

The ultimate in weaving freedom is obtained when both the warp and the weft are freed from all restraint. This is the way in which weaving is following and in many cases passing free expression modes in other artistic fields. The technique is only slightly related to traditional weaving but good design requires that nothing is achieved by forcing, what may possibly be called thread sculpture, too far away from normal weaving. The results sought are purely communicative in character, being produced to explain an emotion or a thought as a decorative mural or a hanging panel.

Such a hanging panel is normally made to hang free, usually with a rigid bar at the top or bottom, but even this is too much restraint for some of the more radical of modern artists who feel that the way a panel is displayed is satisfactory provided the decorative effect is achieved. A

Figure 6.5

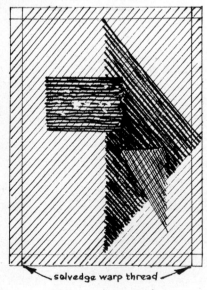

solvedge warp thread

diagonal warp weaving

Figure 6.6

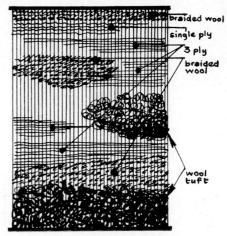

braided wool
single ply
3 ply
braided wool

wool tuft

hanging free form woven panel

hanging panel is woven on a loom and uses more conventional methods than free form murals which are set in a permanent frame. An example of a hanging free form panel is shown as *Figure 6.6* and discussed below.

Hanging Free Form Woven Panels

Figure 6.6 shows a not too radical type of free form hanging panel. There is nothing at all new in the techniques used and the steps for making such a panel are as follows:

(1) A tapestry loom is set up as described in Chapter 5 with the exception that the bridle sticks at the back of each beam are replaced by the permanent bars which then become part of the panel.

(2) The warp threads are part of the design and must be allowed for in choosing the thread for the warp and in the way the warp is rigged. In the example all of the warp threads are equally spaced and parallel but an artist may feel that his particular design may be better served by grouped warps or by warps running non-parallel. If such is the case this decision is possibly most conveniently made at the time of setting up the loom, although in such a free expression endeavour extra warp threads may be added almost as an after-thought.

(3) With the warps in place and properly tensioned, weaving can begin. It may be found that a second shed stick taking the place of the leash stick is a more convenient way of working.

(4) Any material may be woven into the article to create the design which may have been decided upon before work commenced, or more likely, is allowed to grow as the inclination of the artist dictates.

(5) Threads can be plaited, braided, woven into strips or otherwise treated before being incorporated in the design. The pattern in *Figure 6.6* was chosen more from the point of view of simplicity and to demonstrate a variety of textural surfaces than for artistic merit.

(6) The essence of free form weaving is that it *be* free form, not bound by mundane requirements or possible utility value but purely as a medium in which artistic creativity and imagination can be passed on to others.

The above brief discussion does not do justice to the possibilities of the above type of expression, but it should open to the adventurous an avenue of artistic exploration that is truly exciting.

Thread Murals

In freeing weaving from its conventional concepts, we have dispensed with the warp as such and then freed the weft. Now to divorce all tradition away from the technique to be discussed, the loom itself is to be discarded. It may be that there are little, if any, normal weaving techniques left but in its place there are the most exciting, the most challenging possibilities in free creative expression yet offered in this book. Consider *Figure 6.7* where there is illustrated a panel highly appropriate to a contemporary decorative scheme and bearing some resemblance to conventional weaving. It is carried out entirely in homespun, natural coloured wool, set in a white-wood naturally finished frame. The semi-circle is made from braided (flat plaited) wool thread. The details of the construction can be generally

Figure 6.7

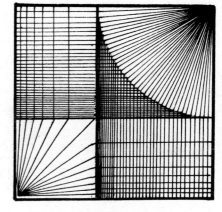

thread mural

Figure 6.8

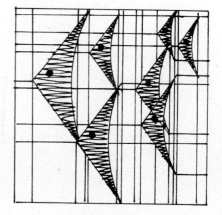

thread mural

Figure 6.9

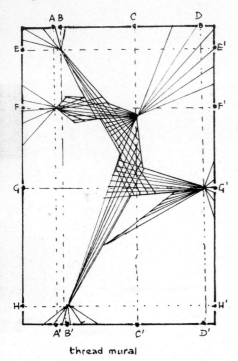

thread mural

Figure 6.10

double mural

seen from the figure. Where the threads touch and change direction they are tied with neutral coloured thread at that point. Similar designs to this are easily conceived and readily carried out. For the most effective results the threads should run through holes drilled through the frame where, after bringing to the desired tension, they can be wedged in the hole with small tapered sticks to which a dab of cement has been applied to make the wedging permanent. A less workmanlike job is to anchor the ends of the threads to small panel pins driven into the rear of the frame.

The mural shown in *Figure 6.8* is an even more striking demonstration of the possibilities inherent in the technique under discussion. In designing a mural of this sort a full-scale pattern, or at least a scaled pattern, should be drawn onto paper in order to allow the framework of threads to be strung in the correct position before the design is woven into place. A fairly substantial frame is needed and it is suggested that for certain types of mural, possibly including the one in *Figure 6.8*, they can well be framed in bamboo. In making the corners of a bamboo frame, the ends should be plugged with close fitting wooden plugs and well cemented into place with an epoxyl resin cement.

In *Figure 6.9* is shown an example which requires threading from one side of the frame to the other and from top to bottom through the position where the points of attachment of the permanent threads will be. In the figure in question, a strong cord will need to run from top to bottom between points marked A1, B, B1, C, C1, and so on in order to temporarily support the outline of the figure until the permanent internal and external threading can be done. In a case such as this, it is imperative that holes be drilled for the permanent threads through the frame and small wedges used in adjusting the tension of the threads. A second person to lend aid in the adjustment of the final tension will be of considerable assistance. It must be allowed that a mural such as the one shown is not easy to execute, but the results achieved will more than compensate for the difficulties of production.

The last example as shown in *Figure 6.10* is a complicated and difficult piece of thread work, but quite within the reach of a careful craftsman. It represents quite an elaborate combination of nearly all the techniques discussed in this chapter. To begin with the canoe is worked on a thread background. This double type of mural gives highly effective two-dimensional effects.

A deep wooden frame is required, most conveniently made in two pieces. The background is worked first, using free weft techniques and carrying the design below the level of the canoe.

The canoe and the foreground is also worked with free weft techniques but in addition the warp is free and suspended with temporary warp cords until a suitable framework of diagonal and straight warp threads is laid down to carry the weft sufficiently well to hide all of the warp. Finally, the spiral embellishments are worked into the surface as a raised pattern, or spirals made of plaited wool thread can be caught to the surface with neutral coloured thread.

Elaborate though the production may be, this type of free weaving is certainly effective and not obtainable in any other way.

Creative Weaving

This chapter set out to show that weaving, when regarded without reference to the long years of tradition that support conventional methods, is a medium in which the most talented artist-craftsman can find new horizons, new challenges and the opportunities of achieving results far different from those normally regarded as the field of the weaver. It is hoped that the suggestions offered above will result in many beginners and experienced weavers alike attempting some of the highly imaginative and creative techniques discussed.

CHAPTER SEVEN

Weaving patterns and choosing a loom

'Tis said that there is merit in a man taking time to choose wisely in taking unto himself a wife. This advice is equally valid when applied to a crafter in choosing a loom.

There are many types of looms offering either for sale in a built-up form or as plans for a handyman to make. Each type of loom employs more or less the same principle of operation and they all produce more or less the same material with one set of threads interlocking a second set of threads lying at right angles. All this has been well discussed in Chapter 4, but the time has come when a more critical look must be taken at the differences which exist between the various styles of looms in order that a wise crafter can choose a loom with care.

The Choice of a Loom

So many variations in looms have been developed that it is difficult to divide types of looms into any sort of logical order, but they can be roughly grouped as to their capabilities. First it may be as well to mention the three factors that are the prime factors influencing an individual choice These can be considered as under:

(1) The type of material that it is desired to produce. It would indeed be a strange person who welcomes complications simply for the sake of complication, for quite innocently, beginners in the art of weaving very often act in this way. Presumably they are carried away with the glowing description of a certain loom that they have purchased at a high price, a loom capable of handling the most complex of patterns, yet they never feel the need to master the intricacies of their loom. Hence they continually work an expensive and bulky loom to a fraction of its capacity when they would have been much more conveniently served with a smaller and less costly machine. To avoid this trap is not easy, for how can one positively decide at the beginning of a career as a weaver what the ultimate aim may be. However, it must be taken into account that experience can be gained on a simple loom and when the need arises, this loom can be disposed of in favour of a more elaborate piece of equipment. As a general rule it can be taken that any loom which is described as being of greater complexity than 'a four-way loom' should be very carefully considered before purchasing. The significance of the term 'four-way' will become apparent in this chapter and one of the aims of this book is to explain the very great range of possibilities in weaving, using nothing more complex than a four-way loom; a type of loom which is neither complex nor very expensive.
(2) The space for the storage of a loom: Two general factors influence the amount of room that a loom will take up in a home.

(i) The complexity of the loom and this has been considered in (1) above.
(ii) The width of the material to be woven: Hand looms are used in a number of widths. From the point of view of making the fabric into garments or hangings, the wider the material the easier it is, in general, to use. There is a limit to the distance a hand shuttle can be thrown however,

and this must give an upper limit to the width of cloth produced. The width to which an individual can throw a shuttle will vary from weaver to weaver and it is common to find the more complicated looms fitted with a semi-automatic foot powered shuttle-throwing device that will allow very fast weaving of considerable width, but it is felt that such looms are beyond the scope of the true amateur. As a generalisation, and there seems to be a lot of these in this section, looms of from 24 inches to 30 inches wide are a convenient choice. Much wider, and there is trouble in moving them from room to room, although this difficulty can be overcome by a folding pattern loom. To produce cloth for general purposes of lesser width than a 24 inch loom will make, will create difficulty in the making up of garments and other woven goods from the narrow cloth produced. A further limitation on very wide looms is the somewhat tedious chore of laying the warp. It is not unusual to have warps of 25 dents to the inch and a four-foot loom threaded with that number of warps would take hours of painstaking work, with the result that the weaver will be tempted to use only part of the width anyway.

(3) The cost of the loom: Obviously there will be a very great variation in the price of looms in accordance with the degree of complexity, the size, and other factors. It is fair to say that much thought and some understanding in analysing one's needs should take place before making a final selection.

The above covers what one may consider to be the basic factors to be taken into account in choosing a weaving loom. Further data will come only from a closer study of the function of looms in the production of particular types of cloth and this is considered now.

Weaves
There are only a limited number of changes which can be incorporated into weaving to alter the fabric produced.

(1) The choice of thread: The choosing of the weaving thread, whether it be woollen, cotton, silk, linen, artificial fibre, or any other of the great multitude of fibres which have at one time or another been turned into cloth, is something which with very special exceptions, is independent of the type of loom employed in the weaving.

(2) The combination of various materials: The textural quality of a piece of woven material is changed by introducing new thread into the weaving pattern. The number of different threads that may be introduced and the order in which they are introduced is a direct function of the type and complexity of the loom.

(3) The choice of colour: Quite obviously the colour of a given thread will not affect the operation of a loom and this does not need to be taken into account.

(4) Combinations of colour will be subject to the type of loom used as with combinations of material in (2) above.

(5) Variations in the thickness of the thread being used will (within a very wide range of thickness) not be of any very great account in choosing a loom. This is particularly true in the case of the weft thread.

(6) The fineness of the fabric: In theory, any loom can carry an unlimited number of warp threads to each inch of width, but it is obvious that there must be a limit to the number of heddle leashes or loops which can be fitted into a given space on a given loom. However, this is not likely to be of any great moment for few modern hand-loom weavers would care to emulate the feat of the court weaver to Queen Isabella (a medieval Queen of Italy) who was ordered by his Queen to produce a cloth of gossamer woven at 140 threads to the 'pollice' which is very nearly equivalent to our inch. Certainly no inexperienced weaver is likely to find that a moderate size modern loom will fail to carry the required number of warp threads per inch.

At this point it may be wise to summarise the above to discover which of the particular items discussed need to be further considered.

(1) Choice of thread – does not affect the choice of loom.
(2) Combinations of thread – *does* affect the choice of loom.
(3) Colour – does not affect the choice of loom.
(4) Colour combination – *does* affect the choice of loom.
(5) Thickness of thread – does not affect the choice of loom.
(6) Fineness of the fabric – does not affect the choice of loom.

It appears that, within wide enough limits to suit all weaves with the exception of those with special requirements, there are only two factors in the actual weave which will be pertinent to consider in choosing a loom suited to one's particular needs. These two factors are both concerned with the way in which the weft is laid in, with respect to the warp.

Let us refer back to Chapter 4 for a moment and give thought to what was said there in regard to forming the shed through which the shuttle passes to lay the weft. It becomes apparent after a little reflection, that whichever threads are lifted depends on the way the warp is threaded through the heddle leashes. Changing patterns by changing the order in which the weft interlocks with the warp creates a problem as to which way the heddles are to be tied and the order in which these heddles open the shed.

The above is the crux of the whole question of pattern weaving and the reason for so many different types of looms and the complexity of looms designed to handle intricate patterns. To understand the way in which different types of cloth are produced is to be well on the way towards handling a loom intelligently and, with understanding, the ability to set a loom to produce the material required.

In order to understand how weaves are developed, the section immediately below considers an elementary type of loom, well within the capabilities of any crafter to make and one on which a great variety of weaving patterns can be produced in a simple, inexpensive way. It is felt that to learn by doing, is worth many many pages of discussion and it is strongly suggested that all beginners and the majority of moderately experienced weavers will profit by building and experimenting with the miniature loom described below. It may be added that the results of experiments on this elementary loom are capable of useful application, as will in turn be shown.

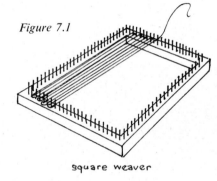

Figure 7.1

square weaver

Building a Square Weaver
The simple piece of apparatus shown in *Figure 7.1* is designed for the weaving of four inch squares of cloth in a great number of alternative patterns. As can be seen from the figures, the weaver consists of a square frame and a number of steel pins on which woollen thread is strung. The construction of the weaver is as follows:

Materials Required –
4 pieces of dressed soft wood – 5 × ½ × ½ inches.
62 headless pins ¾ inch long (Panel pins with the heads nipped off after driving will replace the headless pins.)
1 five or six inch straight steel needle.
A quantity of woollen thread.

Construction –
The four pieces of wood are glued and pinned to form a square. It is important that the corners remain square and details of the type of joint that will ensure this are given in *Figure 7.2*. The pins must be carefully spaced and driven well into the soft timber. Soft timber, pine or bass is needed to avoid splitting which might occur with a line of pins driven into harder timber. The pattern in which the pins are driven is as follows:

(i) A pin is driven into the centre of each of two diagonally opposite corners.
(ii) Space 15 pins at ¼ inch spacing down the centre line of each side.

The square weaver is ready for use.

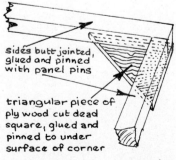

Figure 7.2

sides butt jointed, glued and pinned with panel pins

triangular piece of ply wood cut dead square, glued and pinned to under surface of corner

detail of corner construction

To String a Square Weaver

(i) The weaver is placed on a table with one of the corner pins in the lower left-hand corner as the operator faces the weaver.

(ii) Tie the thread to the above pin and string the weaver by carrying the thread back and forth around each pin in turn until all nails are filled and there are 15 loops top and bottom of the weaver. This operation is shown partly completed in *Figure 7.1*.

(iii) The warp laying is completed by tieing off to the other corner pin diagonally opposite the starting pin.

(iv) Wind thread eight times around the outside of the nails in order to measure off the necessary length of weft thread.

(v) The weft is wound to a loose ball until ready to commence weaving. Woollen thread must always be wound loosely to avoid straining the thread.

(vi) The long needle is threaded and the weaver is ready for weaving.

Tabby or Plain Weave

(i) Pass the needle under the outside warp thread, over the next thread, under the next and so on and finally take it around the first pin.
This instruction can be written:

Row 1 – U1, O2, U3, O4, U5, O6, . . . end U15
Row 2 – O14, U13, O12, U11, O10, . . . end U1
Row 3 – O2, U3, O4, U5, O6, U7, . . . end U15
Row 4 – O14, and repeat 2nd row
Thus continue to 15th row.

This pattern is shown again in *Figure 7.3*.

Note that the odd number of warp threads causes the weft to pass in the same direction under the outside warp threads to provide a firm selvedge. This is considered to be good practice. After each weft is laid, push it back into place to line with the appropriate pin around which the weft has been passed.

(ii) The completed square is eased off the pins and the beginning and end of the weft woven into the selvedge.

The tabby weave square can be laid aside for later comparison with other weaves. This comparison becomes easier if different coloured warp and weft threads are used.

Tabby weave is the basic weave and even the most complicated loom 'set-ups' are always rigged so as to allow of tabby weave being done. In most patterns tabby is used to begin and end a pattern.

Figure 7.3   Figure 7.4

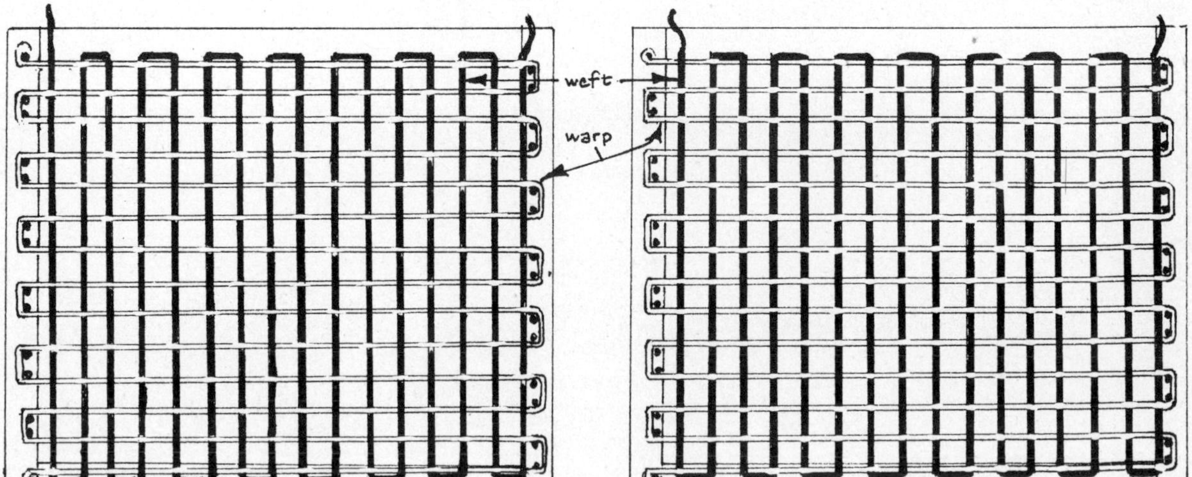

tabby weave   twill weave

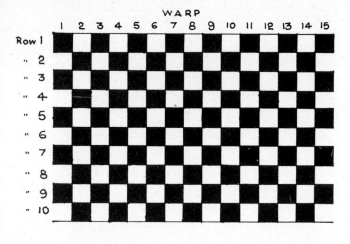

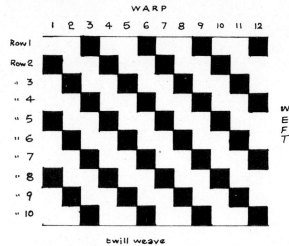

Plain or tabby weave   twill weave

Figure 7.6   *Figure 7.8*

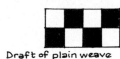

Draft of plain weave

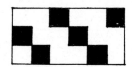

draft of twill weave

Variations on Tabby Weave (Colour and Texture)

Without changing the basic tabby weaving pattern of over one, under one, etc, colour patterns can be introduced. For instance a black and white check pattern can be woven thus:

(i) In stringing the warp, string three lengths of black yarn as normal and instead of returning for the fourth run, omit three pins so that the next three lengths are not run and then string the next three lengths and so on.

(ii) Begin with the white yarn, missing the first three sets of pins, fill in the missing lengths and continue as with the black.

The result will be alternative bands of black and white warp thread.

(iii) Run off $\frac{1}{2}$ wefts and thread up two needles, one with black and one with white thread.

(iv) Run three rows of black weft, then 3 rows of white weft and so on, using generally the same technique as discussed under tabby weaving.

(v) The loose ends must all be woven into the selvedge on completing the square.

A large number of different colour patterns can be woven by using more than two colours, changing the width of the band and so on. Textural patterns can also be produced by using different thicknesses of threads or different materials to form the pattern.

It is interesting to consider that Scottish tartans can be produced from a simple tabby weave and this is described in Chapter 9. However, unless the square weaver is made a good deal larger than 4 inches, it does not allow enough room for the development of representative tartans. It should also be mentioned that traditionally Scottish tartans were produced in a 'twill' weave (which is the next weave to be discussed in this section), but few weavers today find the complications of combining twill weaving techniques with the number of colour changes required for the more complicated tartans to be worth the additional trouble.

Figure 7.9

Irish chain weave

Twill Weave

The twill weave has a more distinctive pattern than plain weave. Twill is the second of the basic weaves as used to create distinct surface textures on fabric. Twill is woven in the following way:

Row 1 – O1, O2, U3, O4, O5, U6, O7, O8, U9, . . . end U15
Row 2 – O14, U13, O12, O11, U10, O9, O8, U7, . . . end U1
Row 3 – U2, O3, O4, U5, O6, O7, U8, O9, . . . end O15
Row 4 – O1, O2, U3, and continue as for Row 1
Row 5 – As for Row 2
Row 6 – As for Row 3
and continue rows to end of square in the same sequence.

Changes of colour and texture can be introduced into the twill weave pattern as with the tabby weave.

The characteristic diagonal lines of twilled fabric are given by the moving sideways of the double jump of the weft thread over the warp. This is shown in *Figure 7.7* in comparison to *Figure 7.5* showing the plain or tabby weave.

Pattern Drafting

For many reasons, most of which are fairly obvious, it is desirable to plan a weaving pattern on paper before work is commenced. The majority of experienced weavers have either devised their own system or adopted traditional methods of displaying their weaving patterns and beginners can find this one of the more confusing aspects of weaving. Actually, the drafting of a pattern is not a difficult task and indeed, the basic patterns for both tabby and twill weaving have been done in the discussion on those two fundamental weaves as given above and shown in *Figure 7.6* and *7.8*.

It is to be noticed that drawn out on graph or squared paper:

(1) The horizontal rows of squares represent weft threads, each row representing one pass of the shuttle through a shed. Some weavers refer to the laying down of a single weft thread as a 'pick'. Thus 3 picks will mean the laying down of 3 consecutive threads. So we can restate thus – each horizontal row of squares in the pattern draft represents one pick.
(2) The vertical rows of squares represent the warp threads, each row representing one thread. Single warp threads are sometimes called 'warp ends', so again restating – each vertical row represents one warp end.
(3) The solid squares and the open squares give reference to the position of the pick (weft thread) with reference to the warp end at that cross-over.
(4) A solid square means the weft in that row crosses under the warp end of that row; an open square that the weft moves over the warp. Refer to *Figure 7.5* and take a solid square at random – say the square showing the cross-over at weft row five, warp row eight. This square is solid so the weft goes under the warp, whereas in weft row three, warp row eleven, the square is shown open and the weft passes over the warp.

(5) It is only necessary to show sufficient of a pattern draft to mark off one pattern unit. If *Figure 7.6* is studied in comparison to *Figure 7.5* it is seen that repeating *Figure 7.6* enough times will give *Figure 7.5* and that this procedure can be extended to any size piece of material. Similarly *Figure 7.8* gives the necessary detail to be extended to *Figure 7.7* or any size larger. The next section below uses pattern drafts to explain more complicated patterns than the two previously described.

Combination Weaves

A considerable number of traditional weaving patterns are known and named. Several of these are worth demonstrating on the square weaver as follows:

Figure 7.9: Irish chain weave – it will be noticed that the more complicated designs introduce what is referred to as 'overshots' which can be defined as threads which pass over the warp to make the pattern. It can be seen from the draft of the Irish chain that there are series of three undershots continually repeated. To produce too many overshot threads in one's work is poor design and this should be guarded against. In all cases, the actual pattern design should be set off with tabby weave and in drafting a pattern it is assumed that tabby weaving backs up the design in every direction.

Figure 7.10: The long chain demonstrates a border design.
Figure 7.11: The Stairs to Heaven is a traditional South Seas' native design.

It is strongly suggested that a square weaver be made and be used for the purpose of pattern experiments. Although the size does limit the complexities of the patterns that can be developed, it is so quick and easy to string that a pattern can be tried out in a number of variations and colour combinations in a very short time. And that raises the question of the choice of colours to use together.

Colour Combinations

It must be remembered that when a pattern is developed using two colours there will be two separate colour effects if the combination is an intimate one as is the case when one colour is used as a warp and another for the

Figure 7.10

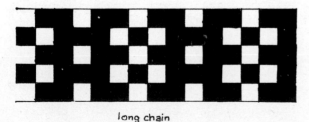

long chain

Figure 7.11

"Poutama" – stairs to Heaven

weft. Both of these effects will have to be considered apart in most cases. They are:

(1) The close-up effect in say a dress fabric or drape when the observer is standing close enough for both threads to register.

(2) The effect which appears at a sufficient distance for the two colours to blend together, giving the appearance of a third colour. This phenomenon is well enough known but sometimes overlooked until too late to remedy.

(a) White will lighten a colour by several shades depending on the proportion of white to the other colour.

(b) Similarly, black will darken a colour but unless used sparingly, will give a muddy depressing cast to the shade. It is difficult to preserve a sparkling look to a shade where black has been used in the make up.

(c) The following colour combinations are given as suggestions only, as so much depends on the original shades. In all cases it is wise to weave a square from the proposed threads and check the result. With these reservations, these combinations are given in no particular order:

Dark Brown and Black (very sparingly) ..	Sepia
Dark Brown and Red	Terra Cotta
Dark Brown and Orange	Burnt Ochre
Vermilion and Crimson	Scarlet
Vermilion and Blue	Misty Blue-grey
Crimson and Purple	Magenta
Purple and Indigo	Junior Navy
Green and Yellow	Apple Green
Green and Brown	Olive
Blue and Purple	Ultramarine
Indigo and Greens	A range of blue-greens

The above are samples of the more unlikely combinations, there being dozens of others. These colour combinations are a rich source of interest in experiments with a square weaver.

Practical Square Weaving

The square weaver, especially if enlarged somewhat in size, is a ready and cheap way to do practical weaving, requiring only patience to accomplish some very useful projects. The sample squares in all their variety can be sewn together with matching thread using overlock stitches. After all the squares are formed the completed work can be blocked to shape by covering with a damp cloth and pressing into the desired shape. A few possibilities for using woven squares are given below:

(a) Car rugs and bed covers – woven squares made of odd lengths of knitting wool and left-overs of wool weaving yarn make most economical soft and warm rugs. A woven rug of this type can take less than half of the quantity of material required in producing the same sized article by knitting or crocheting. About 4 yards of woollen thread will make a 4 inch square and with a little practice a rug can be more speedily made in this way than by either knitting or crocheting. Block patterns are an obvious way to embellish such rugs.

(b) Scarves are other useful articles made 2 or 3 squares wide and of any length.

(c) Woven belts offer yet another project for knitted squares and knitting and shopping bags using wooden or plastic handles are a natural use for suitable squares.

A square weaver provides an excellent source of enjoyment for children and is an ideal present for anybody who may be interested in beginning weaving as a craft.

However, it must be remembered that to the serious weaver, the use of a square weaver is mainly for the development of suitable designs and as an introduction to the use of the larger size more productive looms as dealt with in the next chapter.

CHAPTER EIGHT

Setting up the loom

Already it has been shown that highly practical weaving can be done without the need to spend large sums of money on equipment. However, all the equipment so far discussed has lacked the sophistication of design necessary for speedy production of cloth. For the serious weaver who feels the need to produce quantites of hand-woven material of their own manufacture, it is necessary for them to face up to the outlay of a fairly sizable amount of cash in order that they may provide themselves with a suitable loom and associated equipment.

At the risk of offending many who have had notable success with simpler types of looms, let it be said as serious advice that to purchase a loom which will not allow a fairly wide range of patterns to be woven is to prejudice the opportunities for really creative work. This immediately dismisses a wide range of simple looms, the most notable of which and possibly the most useful is the 'rigid heddle' loom of which more shall be said later. The rigid heddle loom is worth special mention for there may be those who have decided that creative pattern weaving does not interest them and they will be fully content with tabby weaving and the variations in colour and texture patterns which arise from tabby weaving.

At the risk of offending a further group of weavers let it be said that until the weaver personally feels the need for an elaborate loom, he or she should not yield to the temptation of purchasing any loom more complicated than a four shaft loom. As this suggestion is almost sure to raise some criticism it may be wise to discuss the types of weaving that can be accomplished on a four shaft loom even though the meaning of what is stated in the term 'four shaft' has not yet been given.

Capabilities of Four Shaft Looms

The following traditional weaves are possible using four shaft looms, or if the traditional pattern is not exactly reproduced, a perfectly satisfactory version of the weaves mentioned below can be woven using only four shafts:

(i) The whole group of plain or tabby weaves including tartans, simple brocades, fine suiting and many more.
(ii) Twills.
(iii) Tweeds (of which more is said in a section towards the end of this chapter).
(iv) All-over texture weaves including honeycomb, canvas, and huck-a-back.
(v) Simplified crepe weaves, piques, whipcords, Bedford cords and corduroys.
(vi) Simple modifications of a four shaft loom will allow gauze and velvet to be woven.

Plus many many more weaves, including combinations of the above, thus giving special pattern effects.

In fairness it should also be stated that a four shaft loom will not allow the following weaves to be woven:

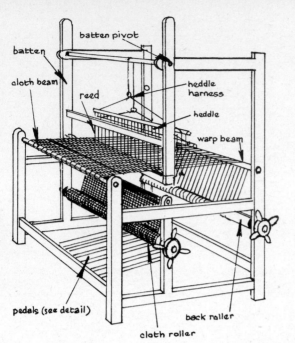

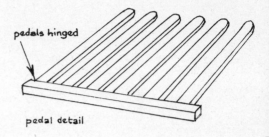

batten pivot

batten

cloth beam

reed

heddle harness

heddle

warp beam

Figure 8.1

pedals hinged

pedal detail

pedals (see detail)

back roller

cloth roller

4 shaft, 6 pedal foot pedal

(i) Many of the linen weaves.

(ii) All of the damasks and this to many advanced weavers is a cardinal point, for among the block patterns of damask are some of the most challenging of weaving patterns. However, beginners should not feel too bad about not being able to start in doing damask weaving for one of the most popular in this class of pattern requires a twenty harness – twenty-four pedal loom and that is quite a hand loom.

Foot or Table Looms

There is no question of the superiority of a foot loom over a hand operated table loom. About all that can be said in favour of a table loom is that it takes up less storage space and is cheaper to buy. In almost every other respect the foot operated loom is superior to the table loom. It is worth-while considering some of these advantages as under:

(i) Quite obviously if the feet provide some of the movements needed in weaving, one's hands are freer to get on with the job of passing the shuttle through the shed.

(ii) As one of the advantages of a table loom is the small space it occupies when stored, it must also follow that as a general rule there is less space inside a table loom than in a floor model. This is important for a number of reasons. Reference to *Figure 8.1* shows that the length of warp from the back roller to in front of the reed where the weaving is actually carried out is comparatively long. A table model if it is to be a reasonable size, has not the space to allow the same length of warp. Yet the longer the warp, within reason, the less strain there is when making a shed and therefore the tension on individual warp ends tends to remain unchanged; there are less broken warp threads and the weaving is more even. In addition, an open type of loom is far easier to work inside when setting up than a more cramped table model.

(iii) A more technical point is the action of the batten which carries the reed to beat the weft back into place after each pass of the weft thread (each pick). In *Figure 8.1* the batten is slung (pivotted) from above. It is said to be overslung. In the majority of table looms (again in order to keep the size down) the batten is pivotted below the warp. In this position it is said to be underslung. There are at least two advantages of overslung battens versus underslung:

(1) An underslung batten tends to fall forward into the 'fell' (the fell is the edge of the cloth where the last pick was beaten in), in the action of beating the weft. This makes for a tiring hand movement when it is necessary to hold the batten back during the longer strokes of the batten at the beginning of weaving so as to maintain the same force as will be applied when the fell gets nearer to the reed, as more cloth is woven. It should be realised that the weaving action continues from the cloth beam inward towards the reed and the more weft woven in, the less the distance between the fell and the reed and so the movement of the reed in beating becomes less as weaving proceeds.

(2) An overslung batten swings forwards and upwards and the fell is easily visible at all points of the swing. An underslung batten swings forward and downwards and especially at the beginning of weaving when the batten stroke is long, the reed hides the fell.

There are other even more technical reasons for the superiority of foot operated looms over table looms but sufficient should have been said to display the wisdom of purchasing a floor model loom in preference to a table model. If lack of space is a critical factor it should be remembered that a well finished loom is quite acceptable as a piece of decorative furniture in any home, and folding looms are quite practical.

The Weaving Action
If the discussion in Chapter 4 on the general principles of weaving and the consideration given above to the advantages of a number of the actions of a foot powered loom have been followed, a fair general under-standing of the operation of the loom in *Figure 8.1* should be known. However, for the sake of clarity and at the risk of being repetitious let us run over the weaving action and then 'get down to cases' in more detailed discussion of the four-way principle.

The process of weaving on a loom such as that depicted in *Figure 8.1* is as follows:

(1) Warp threads are strung from the adjustable back roller over the warp beam through the heddle loops, through the reed, over the cloth beam and are attached to the adjustable cloth roller.

(2) One set of heddles is caused to rise and the warp threads which are threaded through those particular heddles are lifted as well; the remaining heddles and the rest of the warp remaining in their original position. (Any variation on this simple heddle action is left for later discussion.)

(3) A shed is formed by the separation of the two sets of warp threads and through this shed a shuttle is thrown, paying out a weft thread behind the shuttle.

(4) The batten is swung down and the reed slides parallel to the warp carrying the weft into place and beating it in.

(5) The opposite set of heddles are then caused to rise and through the new shed a new pick is made.

(6) When the fell has advanced too close to the reed to allow of easy shuttle action, the back roller is slackened off, unrolling extra warp, while the cloth roller winds part of the finished cloth onto itself, thus moving the fell forward and restoring tension to the warp.

Consider then the rhythmical action involved in weaving a tabby pattern cloth:

(i) The first set of heddles (held in a heddle frame as in *Figure 8.2*) rises, lifting half the warp threads and the first shed is formed.

(ii) The shuttle is thrown say from right to left through the shed.

(iii) The heddle frame is lowered.

(iv) The batten is swung forward and the last pick is beaten into the fell by the reed.

(v) The second set of heddles is caused to rise and carry the alternative warp threads upwards and open the second shed.

(vi) The shuttle is thrown from left to right.

(vii) The heddle frame is lowered.

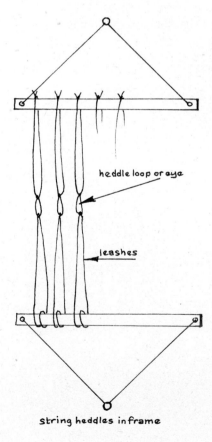

Figure 8.2

heddle loop or eye

leashes

string heddles in frame

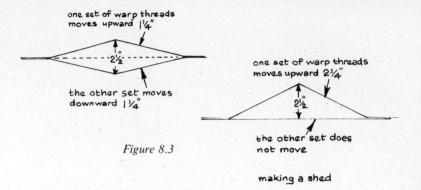

one set of warp threads
moves upward 1¼"

2½

the other set moves
downward 1¼"

one set of warp threads
moves upward 2¼"

2½

the other set does
not move

Figure 8.3

making a shed

Figure 8.4

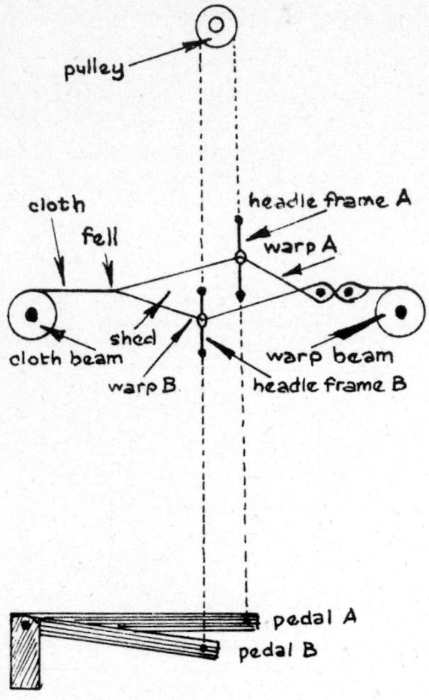

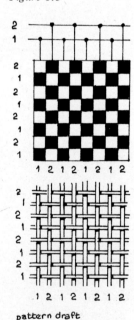

two-way loom action

Figure 8.5

pattern draft
and weave "tabby"

(viii) The batten is swung forward and the last pick is beaten in.
(ix) The action from (i) to (viii) is repeated.

It is emphasised that the weaving procedure involves a rhythmical action with hands, feet and loom working together.

Now let us have a look at the one feature that has not as yet been discussed in detail – the raising of the heddle frames.

Two-way Action

Fairly obviously the movement of the heddles is controlled by the action of the foot operated pedals in the case of the loom shown in *Figure 8.1*. No great difficulty would be experienced in tying one end of a cord to the end of the pedal, over a pulley above the heddle frame and on to the harness above the heddle frame. When the pedal was depressed the heddle would rise. However, let us give consideration to the making of a shed. The warp threads have to be pulled far enough apart to allow room for the shuttle to pass through. At the same time the warp threads need to be subject to the smallest amount of movement, thus reducing the strain on the warp. If one set of warp threads moves upwards while the opposite set moves downward, each thread will need to move only half the distance to make a shed of a certain size, compared to the distance the individual threads would move for the same size shed if only one set of threads were moved. *Figure 8.3*.

In order to reduce to a minimum the amount of strain on the warp it is usual to set up a loom with two heddles (a loom with two heddles will only make tabby and variations on tabby weaves) as shown in *Figure 8.4*.

The two-way action of the loom shown diagramatically as *Figure 8.4* is clearly shown in the figure.

Threading Order – Two Way

The two-way action with two foot pedals makes for fast weaving of tabby or plain weaves. However, let us think back to the last chapter and some of the patterns woven on the square weaver. It will be recalled that most of the pattern weaving required tabby weaving in one part of the pattern and a change to another weave for another section of the weaving.

Let us consider how this can be shown on a pattern draft. With reference to *Figure 8.5* it can be seen that the pattern draft shown there includes the following:

(i) The blocked squares represent the warp threads which pass through heddle eyes.
(ii) The two lines at the top represent the heddle frames.
(iii) The vertical lines above the draft show the ties between the warp threads and the heddle frames.

Note – This is only one of the several ways a pattern draft shows the 'tie up' between threads and heddle frames and most other ways of showing pattern drafts are adaptations of the drafts shown here.

Figure 8.6   Figure 8.7   Figure 8.8   Figure 8.9

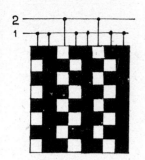

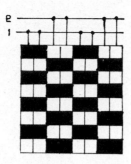

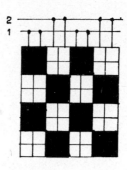

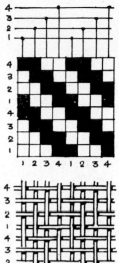

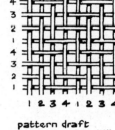

pattern draft
and weave "twill"

The pattern draft in *Figure 8.5* shows the need for only two heddle frames and hence two pedals. With the tie up in *Figure 8.5*, plain tabby weave (as shown under the pattern draft) is woven.

Still using only two heddle frames but with different tie ups, variations on tabby weaves can be woven. *Figure 8.6* shows one such tie up and it may be of interest to carry out this pattern on the square weaver.

Figure 8.7 shows yet another variation possible and this draft is followed by *Figure 8.8* which shows a change in the woven pattern between *Figures 8.7* and *8.8*, but with identical tie ups, the change in pattern being executed by beating two picks into the same shed.

A number of other variations in pattern with two heddle frames are possible and it is an interesting exercise to experiment on paper and see how many variations are possible, limiting oneself to, say, a maximum of three overshot threads in drafting the patterns.

Threading Order – Four Way

Figure 8.9 shows the pattern draft and the weave known as twill weave. Twill weave was one of the examples discussed in Chapter 7. In this figure it is seen that four heddle frames are required for the pattern and the tie up between the warp threads and the heddle frames are shown in the draft. From the draft the following instructions can be obtained:

(i) The first warp thread is tied to heddle frame 1.
(ii) The second warp thread is tied to heddle frame 2.
(iii) The third warp thread to frame 3.
(iv) The fourth to frame 4.
(v) And this order is followed across the full width of the warp. There is still the tie between the heddle frames and the pedals.

There are two points to remember in deciding the connection between the heddle frames and the pedals:

(i) As one frame rises a corresponding one must drop to form the shed fully. (This is technically termed a differential shed action.)
(ii) A loom must always weave tabby in addition to any other pattern.

With these two points in mind, *Figure 8.9* is examined. To weave tabby, frames 1 and 3 must rise and frames 2 and 4 must drop. So frames 1 and 2 are tied in as *Figure 8.10* and frames 2 and 3 likewise. If each frame is tied to the corresponding numbered pedal, then:

(i) Press down pedals 1 and 3 and then 2 and 4 will allow tabby weaving.
(ii) Press down in order pedals 1 and 2; 2 and 3; 3 and 4; 4 and 1 in pairs and then repeating will produce twill pattern.

However, reference to *Figure 8.10* will show that with the arrangement shown in that figure, frames 1 and 2 cannot rise together; neither can frames 3 and 4. Additional arrangements are needed, one such arrangement incorporating 'heddle horses' is shown in *Figure 8.11*. Study of this figure will show that an almost unlimited combination of the four heddle

Figure 8.10

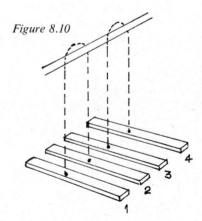

Figure 8.11

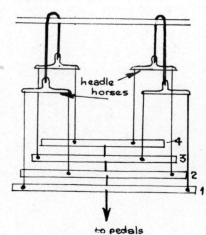

heddle
horses

to pedals

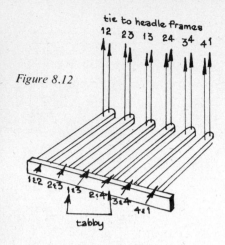

Figure 8.12

tie to headle frames
12 23 13 24 34 41

1&2 2&3 1&3 2&4 3&4 4&1

tabby

Figure 8.13

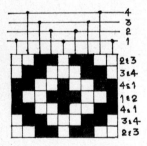

rose path draft

Figure 8.14

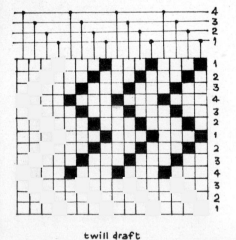

Figure 8.15

twill draft

frames is possible, allowing of a large number of patterns to be woven.

As was said above, there has been much ingenuity expended in arranging the making of a shed for pattern weaving. The way your particular loom is arranged may not appear to 'line up' with the above description but the principle will be the same and any difference will be in detail only.

The way in which the pedals are tied to the heddle frames is shown in *Figure 8.12*. It will be noticed that the two centre pedals are used for tabby weaving.

If a full understanding of the points given above is gained, even comparatively inexperienced weavers will be able to develop any pattern within the capabilities of their own looms. There are many traditional patterns in weaving. For instance, one of the patterns drafted in the next section, the Rose-Path, is of very great antiquity and is yet very popular with today's weavers. However, there are combinations of patterns and textures which will be entirely original and well within the scope of weavers willing to experiment. Drafting patterns on paper, working out the threading and tie up combinations can be highly creative. There are one or two points which must be watched when laying out a draft on to the loom:

(i) A selvedge is needed where patterns are being woven. This means extra threads on the outside of the warp.

(ii) In most cases it is necessary to weave several picks of plain tabby before beginning to weave patterns and the same at the end of the run.

(iii) Allowance must be made to centralise the pattern and for this purpose the pattern should be worked out from the centre of the warp.

Sample Drafts

The patterns which the drafts show in *Figures 8.13* to *8.16* are not given in order that they be used as the basis for actual weaving, but as examples of drafts prepared and given in full detail. Nearly all the information necessary to set the patterns up on a loom are contained in the drafts and as said before this is the starting point for original work. The method of drafting a pattern is simple and fun, and proceeds in this way:

(i) On to a piece of squared paper set out a pattern of filled in squares.

(ii) Watch that the pattern, as laid down, does not include any large number of overshot threads either weft or warp.

(iii) Draw in the threading sequence. To do this successfully, sufficient of the pattern must be displayed to lay out a complete pattern unit as illustrated in both *Figures 8.14* and *8.16*. The other two figures represent overall patterns and could have displayed much less and still have been successful.

(iv) With reference to the pattern and the threading combination, work out and put on the left of the draft the ties which must be made for the heddle frames.

It may well be that in the act of checking operation (iv) it will be found that the threading combination of the pattern is completely impractical for the particular loom available. If this should be the case, changes must be made and the whole process restarted.

Figure 8.16

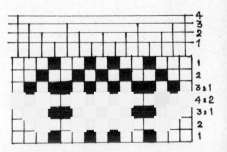

CHAPTER NINE

From thread into cloth

In the same way as 'the proof of the pudding lies in the eating', the success of a weaver rests with 'turning thread into cloth'. In this chapter is given the necessary instructions for dealing with the procedure of setting up a loom and going through all the necessary motions in order that hanks of thread become cloth.

An average sort of a loom has been assumed and while the loom described here may differ in detail from the actual loom in use, it is hoped that sufficient information has already been given for any conflict in the instructions given below and the actual loom being worked on, to be easily resolved. It is also assumed that a very simple article is being woven (in this case, a scarf). However, before work on the loom begins, it may be wise to give consideration to the following.

Traditions
What has to be said about tradition is not easy, but it must be said for much that is confusing in weaving literature lies at the feet of the traditionalist.

First, the technical terms. Many names for loom parts and weaving operations are difficult to follow and there are at least three reasons for this ambiguity and confusion:

(1) The antiquity of the weaving craft so that many terms have medieval or earlier connotations.
(2) The several different sources from which weaving has evolved. Hence there are words from several languages connected with weaving.
(3) The intimate connection between commercial and homecraft weavers. Young tradesman weavers, prior to entry into a full-time working life, are commonly trained on hand looms. They are trained by highly skilled weavers, and are, as a matter of course, introduced to the technicalities of their trade to be, including the technical language which is to become their professional means of communication. All this is very right and proper. The master craftsmen who instruct in the courses of professional weaving write books and articles mainly for the further instruction of fellow professionals to be. This also is very right and proper and of exceedingly great benefit to the general field of weaving. However, the matter does not rest there and it is difficult not to be rueful about this, for these professional master craftsmen produce books that are excellent treatises on their subject and hard to better. However, these books are written in professional language and nominate professional techniques which are completely correct but in many cases entirely beyond the understanding of the amateur, who is however, greatly attracted to them by reason of the excellent information contained therein. Here lies the first difficulty many beginners in weaving run up against.
Secondly, and again because of the professional involvement of many of the most knowledgeable weavers, there tends to be considerable stress on quite complicated weaving methods, particularly in setting up and operating a loom. This is certainly the correct attitude, for once understood,

the correct methods will allow advancement into the most demanding and complex fields of weaving without having to unlearn any faulty (may we say amateurish) ways of doing things.

Commendable as all this may be, it does tend to present a big hurdle and discourage many potential amateur homecrafters from attempting to learn to weave on their own. As this book is offered only as a guide for those who wish to find a way towards making their leisure creative to the fullest possible extent, it has been found necessary to greatly simplify the terms and in some cases, the procedures recommended.

We feel, quite strongly as it happens, that if we be guilty of terminological inexactitudes, then these are fully justified, if, in the process, the procedure has been made easier to follow.

Possibly this should have been said much earlier than in the last chapter but it is particularly relevant now for many of the suggestions about to be made are going to raise cries of horror from the traditionalists, for the suggestions encompass procedures that conflict with methods that authorities stress as particularly important. Our only defence against the charges which are going to be laid is to add that this is a book for the non-professional and the only justification needed for advising some particular method of handling the work, is for that method to work successfully up to the limit of the complexity of what the non-professional homecrafter wishes to undertake.

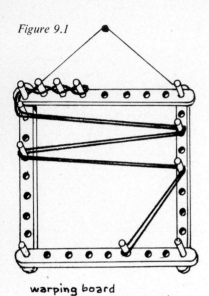

Figure 9.1

warping board
(wall hanging type)

Calculating the Warp

There are many formulae and instructions as to ways of calculating the length of thread needed to make a warp, but as far as most homecrafters are concerned it will be a case of either using what thread is available or readily purchased and then using the most direct commonsense attack on the problem. The most straightforward line of reasoning will likely go:

(i) The width of a scarf – about 10 inches.
(ii) The type of thread – something soft and fluffy, not too hard. A 2 ply wool, say, preferably homespun, fairly loosely twisted.
(iii) Closeness of weave – not too firm, say 12 dents to the inch.
(iv) The number of warp threads:
$$10 \times 12 + 1 \text{ (remember why? Chapter 4)} + 6 \text{ for}$$
$$\text{the average selvedge} = 127$$
(v) The length of the scarf – about five feet.
(vi) The total length of each warp thread $= 60 + 10$ (this extra for the waste between work or tying in etc) $+ 6$ (10% extra on the length which is a fairly generous allowance for the loss of warp length in the process of interlocking with the weft). For the sake of clarity let this be rewritten:
$$60 + 10 + 6 = 6 \text{ ft } 4 \text{ in, more or less.}$$

Six feet four inches may not be a very professional answer but it is not going to make a great deal of difference if the length is out one or two inches either way. Further notes on this subject are given later in this chapter.

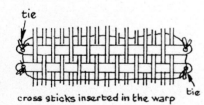

Figure 9.2

tie

cross sticks inserted in the warp   tie

The Warping Board

Figure 9.1 shows a warping board which is constructed as follows:

(1) Four pieces of timber 3 inches by 1½ inches by 3 feet long are needed and about 7 feet 6 inches of 1 inch dowelling are required for the construction as shown in the *Figure 9.1*. The corner pegs hold the frame together and hence it is collapsable for easy storage. This is only one of a number of different devices designed for running off warp threads, most of them capable of handling greater quantities of yarn. However, the warp frame described is highly practical and eminently convenient.
(2) As is shown in the figure, the thread is wound in one piece between the pegs of the frame until a sufficient number of threads of an even length have been wound on to the frame.

(3) In all cases, the starting point must be the four pegs marked in the figure 'A, B, C and D'. The cross-over of the threads between these pegs is essential as is described below.

(4) By moving and selecting the pegs on which the yarn is wound, very exact measurement of warp thread length can be obtained. Gross changes in length are obtained by adjustment of pegs 'E, F, G and H' with perhaps the introduction of extra pegs. Small changes in length are made by shifting peg 'I'.

(5) The simplest way to set up the warping frame pegs to the required length of warp thread is to measure off a piece of yarn to the desired length (in the present instance 6 feet 4 inches) and move the pegs as necessary to accommodate this sample length exactly.

(6) For the scarf, the making of which is being considered, 127 warp threads are wound on to the frame.

(7) Always allow sufficient time to make up the whole warp at one time. This is particularly important with woollen warps in order that the warp threads are all run off under exactly the same conditions and tension.

(8) It is desirable to tie each ten threads into a bundle with a loose tie of wool of a different colour to the warp. This greatly helps subsequent counting of the threads.

Handling Warp

Even 127 threads make quite a bundle and this is a very small warp so that a highly methodical way of handling warp threads must be practised. The suggested procedure is given below:

(i) The cross between pegs 'B 'and 'C' on the warping board in *Figure 9.1* is most important and must never be lost or omitted. The reason for this cross, which incidentally is the 'Porrey Cross' in professional terminology, is shown later in this discussion.

(ii) Two cross sticks are needed. These may be supplied with a loom but if not are easily made. *Figure 9.2* shows two such sticks in their final position in the warp. The material from which the sticks are made is flat or oval section wood, well sanded to avoid snagging the warp, rather longer than the total width of the warp and with a hole drilled near each end. A bridle of strong cord runs from one end hole to the other as shown in *Figure 9.1*. This bridle keeps the sticks in their correct position.

(iii) The cross sticks are placed in the loops on either side of the cross and the bridle tied across to keep the sticks in position. See *Figure 9.3*.

(iv) For easy handling the warp is 'crochetted' as shown in *Figure 9.4*. The crochetted warp should not be pulled tight and the crochetting should be taken to within a foot or so of the cross sticks, which are left in place.

Beaming

Beaming simply means putting the warp on the loom over the beams. There are a number of different ways of doing this, only one of which is mentioned here. Whatever the method adopted, the important phase of the operation is the correct adjustment of the tension of the warp and it may as well be said that this is not at all easy to achieve until some experience has been gained.

(i) The warp is spread on the front or cloth beam of the loom and the cross sticks are tied to the beam using the bridle for this purpose. This is shown as *Figure 9.5*.

(2) Find the centre of the reed and each side of the warp measuring back from the centre and through the dent at this point thread a loop of a warp end. A reed hook of the type shown in *Figure 9.6* is needed and these can either be bought or easily cut from thin plastic sheet.

(3) The heddle frames are lifted and temporarily tied well out of the way and the warp loops are passed through each second dent. That is, a loop is passed through a dent in the reed, the next dent is missed and the next passed through the third dent. A helper makes this job very much easier.

Figure 9.3

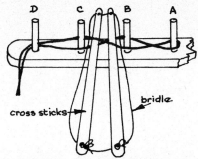

insertion of cross sticks
(the lettered pegs correspond
to the pegs in Fig 9.1)

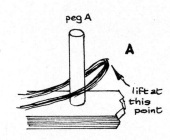

peg A

lift at this point

Figure 9.4

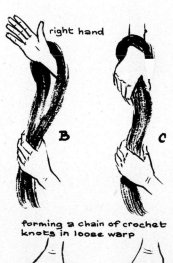

right hand

B   C

forming a chain of crochet knots in loose warp

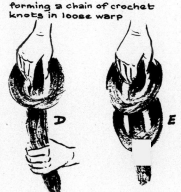

D   E

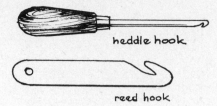

Figure 9.6

heddle hook

reed hook

beaming hooks

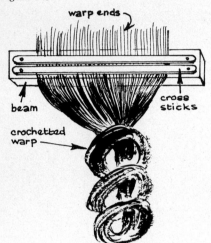

Figure 9.5

warp ends

cross sticks

beam

crochetted warp

(4) Careful attention is paid to the order in which the warp is laid out. By reference to the cross sticks make certain the warp threads are lying parallel.

(5) Consideration must now be given to the warp or back roller. This roller will be fitted with some mechanism that will allow it to turn freely in one direction, but will restrain it from returning in the opposite direction. In all probability this restraining gear will be a pawl and ratchet, somewhat similar to that used on a builder's or ship's winch. In most cases, strong cloth will be attached to the roller so that the action of winding the roller will wind the cloth onto the roller. The front edge of the cloth will be sewn into a pocket which holds a strong wooden rod and to this rod, by means of a series of cord ties, a further wooden rod (the warp rod) will be fastened. *Figure 9.7* has the details.

(6) The warp rod is detached by loosening the cord ties between the rods and each warp loop is in turn slipped over the rod after passing through the reed. When all the warp loops are in place on the rod, attach the rod back to the warp roller cloth by means of the cord ties.

(7) Once again it is absolutely essential to see that the warp is central in respect to the roller cloth and evenly spread the full width of the warp, in this case 10 inches.

(8) The warp must now be wound onto the roller. This is difficult to do alone, so assistance should be sought. A number of warp sticks are needed. These are light, well sanded wooden laths, and they are used to prevent succeeding layers of warp thread on the roller from sinking into the previous layer of thread. The method of using warp sticks is shown as *Figure 9.8.*

(9) Tension must be kept on the loose end of the warp while the warp is being wound, evenly spaced, on to the centre of the warp roller.

(10) As the crochetted warp runs through nearly to the end the cross sticks must be moved close to the warp beam. This is done most easily by using an extra cross stick and turning the original cross stick which lies closest to the reed on its edge, thus producing a shed through which the extra cross stick is fed behind the reed. Push this cross stick to the warp beam, remove the stick from in front of the reed, stand the remaining stick on edge and into the new shed pass the now spare stick. To do this successfully some fair tension must be kept on the warp and the cross sticks should be allowed to come near the reed. Tie the re-positioned cross sticks to the warp beam.

(11) Cut the centre of the front loops of the warp and withdraw them through the reed to leave them hanging loose from in front of the warp beam.

The loom is now set up for 'threading up', 'entering' or 'drawing in' all of which alternative terms means that the warp ends are now to be passed through the appropriate heddles and the reed and be tied to the cloth roller at the front of the loom. There are a few points to recall to mind at this point. The selvedge warp is made from three pairs of doubled warp ends which in the 'threading up' procedure are treated (each pair) as a single warp end passing through the same heddle and reed dent. The threading sequence given so much space in Chapter 8, now becomes of prime importance and the time has come to take a deep breath and a firm determination to keep one's wits entirely on the job. A mistake here is going to mean a very difficult repair job with possible complete re-threading.

The sequence of threading up now continues:

(1) Drop each heddle frame to where it can be conveniently handled.
(2) It is advisable to begin drawing in from the centre of each heddle and certainly essential that the action of each heddle will not cause 'dog legs' or kinks in the straight line of each warp thread.
(3) Adopt some sequence of threading. This is important so that no thread is left free of a heddle or in the wrong place.
(4) The heddle hook is used to draw each warp end through the heddle eye. To date little has been said of the actual heddles and it has been assumed that string heddles are used and indeed they are recommended. Some weavers do prefer wire heddles but it is fair to say, even if it is a fairly general observation, that wire heddles produce more problems than they solve, but are worth trying as the choice rests finally with the individual weaver.
(5) The cloth roller and cloth beam are similar in arrangement to the back roller shown in *Figure 9.7*. The warp ends are tied, usually in bundles of eight on to the cloth stick, which is not removed during this process. The adjustment of warp tension is the critical factor in tying on and this should begin from the centre and work alternatively to the right and left until all the warp is tied on. The preferred knot for this purpose is shown in *Figure 9.9*.
(6) It is impossible to give too much emphasis to the need to have the correct adjustment of warp tension. Tie and re-tie until this is as close to perfect as possible. The quality of the finished weaving depends so very much on strict attention to detail during this operation.

The heddle frames are then attached as was discussed at length in Chapter 8 and the loom is then fully 'dressed' and weaving can commence.

Brick Bats

It is always most discouraging to read at the end of a generally encouraging treatise on a craft, of all the faults that may occur. However, it is even more discouraging to begin weaving and find that 'things are just not going right' and to be at a loss to discover why this should be. Fortunately, the causes of most troubles are fairly obvious, even though most provoking Into this class fall the skipped and missed threads caused by faulty threading. Check the threading carefully to avoid such difficulties.

Nearly all the rest of the troubles are owing to incorrect tensioning. So many difficulties are avoided by looking carefully to the tensioning of the warp that it is worthwhile stating the following points:

Figure 9.7

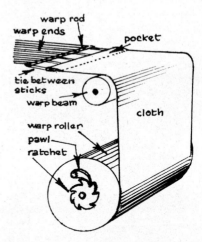

Figure 9.8

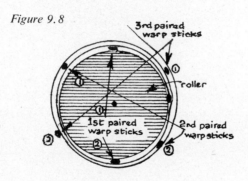

Figure 9.9

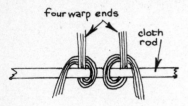

four warp ends

cloth rod

bow

typing on warp

(1) Do not attempt to overload the back roller with too great a length of warp.

(2) Never, but never attempt to use a warp of greater width than the roller.

(3) Wind the warp completely in the one working period.

(4) Beam on all the warp in one working period and tie on similarly.

(5) Always release the tension on the warp when the loom is left if only for a few minutes.

(6) Do not pull the weft in too tight. Waisting of the web is poor weaving technique, looks bad and will inevitably strain the selvedge warp ends.

(7) Handle the warp as seldom as possible.

(8) Beat in firmly with crisp but not heavy blows.

And if the above procedures are carried out with common sense the majority of possible troubles will never show up at all.

Another two fairly common problems arise from carelessness and lack of rhythm in weaving.

(i) Light and dark streaks across the finished material are caused by uneven beating. This was discussed in a previous chapter.

(ii) Skipped warp threads. Careless throwing of the shuttle possibly owing to the throwing being out of time with the pedalling may cause the shuttle to pass over or under the wrong warp threads.

Quantities

So far very little has been said about the weight of thread required for any particular piece of weaving. As might be expected, this is difficult to obtain in most cases, especially where homespun is being used. The strictly practical way of dealing with yarn that is to hand is to run off say fifty yards of the yarn and then weigh this quantity. The fifty yard length can be quickly run off on the warping board. Alternatively, say $\frac{1}{2}$ ounce of yarn may be measured, again by running it off onto the warping board whereupon a simple calculation will yield the length.

Since yarn is generally sold by weight it is also advisable to have at least a rough indication of the relationship between length and weight of common woollen threads, for it is impossible to use the practical method given above, over the shop counter, so to speak.

For this reason the following values are given, the figures are approximate only and it is far better to buy rather more than the calculation would indicate, comforted, we hope, with the thought that wool not used immediately will always come in handy later.

2 ply wool – allow 260 yards per ounce.

3 ply wool – allow 170 yards per ounce.

4 ply wool – allow   60 yards per ounce.

The length of the warp thread will be calculated as given earlier in this chapter. In that calculation there were 127 warp ends each 6 feet 4 inches long.

$$127 \times 6\frac{1}{3} = 806 \text{ feet, say } 269 \text{ yards}$$

The weft, if of the same material as the warp, can be taken as representing about three-quarters of the length of warp thread, or $269 \times \frac{3}{4} = 201$ yards approximately.

Warp plus weft $= 269 + 201 = 470$ yards.

Using 3 ply wool for an example (at 170 yards to the ounce) the weight of wool to be bought, calculated to the nearest $\frac{1}{2}$ ounce above the calculated amount $= 470 \div 170 = 3$ ounces and this leaves a generous amount to spare.

It is interesting to note that this quantity, i.e. 3 ounces of wool for a scarf 5 feet long by 10 inches wide is very much less than the quantity required to knit the same scarf, this bearing out the claim made in Chapter 7 as to the economics of weaving as against other home methods of producing garments.

There remains only the need to give consideration to a few matters that have not fitted well into earlier sections of this book.

Rigid Heddles

It is felt that sufficient justice is not always done to the rigid heddle type of loom. That is, a loom fitted with a rigid metal heddle that acts both as the only heddle frame and a reed, all in one. This simplification allows of a very elementary type of loom, economical to purchase and eminently suited to beginners and for schools and young people's clubs.

Weaving is carried out much as in a normal type of loom, excepting the sheds are made by alternatively raising and lowering the heddle frame. There are two major disadvantages:

(i) There is no differential action in moving the warp for forming a shed as only one set of warps move. This has all the consequent disadvantages discussed in an earlier chapter for this type of action.

(ii) It is essentially a plain weave loom, weaving only tabby and variations of tabby without some adaptations.

Despite the above limitations, the rigid heddle loom must be regarded as much more than a toy. Heddle sticks, as used in tapestry weaving (Chapter 5) can be employed to add a wide variety of patterns to cloth made on a rigid heddle loom. Besides all the variations of tabby, with colour and texture patterns, as discussed elsewhere will give a sufficiency of background to allow a rigid heddle loom to be used to produce material not envisaged by most weavers who condemn a rigid heddle loom as an expensive toy. To use such a loom intelligently requires only imaginative understanding and the will to experiment. Given these a teacher or counsellor for young people will gain much satisfaction in learning and displaying the possibilities of a rigid heddle loom.

Tartans

Scottish tartans represent something special in the lives of many people. It appears that a love of tartan lingers in the hearts of the descendents of Scots long after the love of bagpipe music has been lost. So tartan cloth

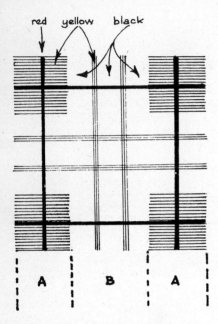

Figure 9.10

red yellow black

A   B   A

McLeod dress tartan

remains ever popular and no book on non-professional weaving can be regarded as being complete without some reference to this most important subject.

Unfortunately, space has become limited in the extreme and far less can be made of tartan weaving than the subject deserves. Traditionally, tartans are twill weaves, but authentic patterns look well in plain weave as produced on a rigid heddle loom.

Tartan Patterns

A detailed study of plaid or tartan patterns shows that in effect two basic patterns are interwoven to obtain the overall effect. To make that statement rather more clear, make reference to *Figure 9.10* which diagramatically shows one of the simplest of all tartans, the McLeod dress tartan. In the figure one pattern is represented as sub-pattern 'A' which is flanked on both sides by sub-pattern 'B'.

Sub-pattern 'A' can be worked out to be:

17 threads yellow		20 threads yellow
2 threads red	and	2 threads red
20 threads yellow		17 threads yellow

– while between the two sections of sub-pattern 'A' lies sub-pattern 'B'.

Sub-pattern 'B':

12 threads black
2 threads yellow
12 threads black
2 threads yellow
12 threads black

These sub-patterns apply to both the warp and weft.

It should be fairly easy to work out any tartan pattern from a sample of the actual tartan cloth or even a photograph. This can be done in the following way. The example selected is the MacKay tartan.

(i) Lay the pattern flat and mark off on to a piece of paper the widths of the various stripes in the pattern. This is shown in *Figure 9.11*.
(ii) The overall width of the pattern in the example is $4\frac{1}{4}$ inches and one point of importance about a tartan is that it must begin and end as a complete pattern. So, assuming a 30 inch loom is available, six complete patterns being $4\frac{1}{4} \times 6 = 25\frac{1}{2}$ inches, would be suited to the loom.
(iii) Assume a fairly fine cloth is required say 24 dents to the inch, then a table can be drawn up in this way:

$\frac{1}{2}$ inch   = 12 threads
$\frac{1}{2}$ inch plus   = say 14 threads
The fine line = say 2 threads

(iv) The warp sequence can then be written down directly from the measurements in *Figure 9.13*:

Green $(\frac{1}{2}^+)$ inches = 14 threads
Black   = 2 threads
Green $(\frac{1}{2}^+)$ inches = 14 threads
Black $(\frac{1}{2})$ inches = 12 threads
Green   = 2 threads
Navy $(\frac{1}{2}^+)$ inches = 14 threads
Green   = 2 threads
Navy $(\frac{1}{2}^+)$ inches = 14 threads
Green   = 2 threads
Black $(\frac{1}{2})$ inches = 12 threads
_____ Repeat
Green $(\frac{1}{2}^+)$ inches = 14 threads
Black   = 2 threads
and so on.

Note that sub-pattern 'A' = 14 green, 2 black, 14 green and sub-pattern 'B' = 12 black, 2 green, 14 navy, 2 green, 14 navy, 2 green, and 12 black. And that the sub-pattern sequence is A, B, A, B, etc ending with an 'A'.

A few more patterns have been worked out in a similar way to the MacKay tartan and are given below:

MacDuff Tartan

This is an interesting plaid pattern as the warp and weft patterns run differently as follows:

Warp A, B, A, B, . . . A
Weft B, A, B, A, . . . B

'A' sub-pattern	'B' sub-pattern
5 Navy	22 Red
5 Black	
8 Green	
6 Red	
2 Black	
6 Red	
2 Black	
6 Red	
8 Green	
5 Black	
5 Navy	

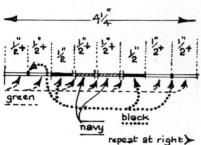

Figure 9.11

repeat at right▶
measurements of Mackay tartan

MacLachlan Tartan

Warp A, B, A, B, . . . A
Weft B, A, B, A, . . . B

'A' sub-pattern	'B' sub-pattern
7 Black	10 Red
10 Navy	2 Black
3 Green	2 Red
10 Navy	2 Black
7 Black	10 Red

MacKenzie Tartan

This is given as one of the class of tartans that departs from the normal interweaving of two patterns for the MacKenzie tartan quite distinctly shows three different sub-patterns:

Warp A, B, A, C, A, B, A, C, A, . . . A
Weft – as the Warp.

'A' sub-pattern	'B' sub-pattern	'C' sub-pattern
8 Green	8 Black	8 Black
2 Black	2 Navy	8 Navy
2 White	2 Black	2 Black
2 Black	2 Navy	4 Red
8 Green	2 Black	2 Black
	8 Navy	8 Navy
	2 Black	8 Black
	2 Navy	
	2 Black	
	2 Navy	
	8 Black	

In measuring off a pattern using the methods described above, some errors are liable to creep in as to the exact width of the stripes, but these should not be gross errors and should not offend any but extreme purists. It is hoped that the above descriptions demonstrate how very easy it is to draft tartan patterns for oneself.

Tweeds

Tweed is a valuable traditional cloth owing more to the treatment given after weaving than to the weaving process itself. True tweeds are nearly all plain or tabby weaves. Springiness and elasticity are typical of good tweeds and the normal rather hairy finish will shed heavy mist or light rain. The openness of the structure (for tweeds are loosely woven) plus the elasticity of the virgin wool used, imparts a considerable amount of snag resistance to tweed clothing in that the fabric will give, rather than tear and then spring back into place when the stress is removed.

True tweed cloth is invariably woven in the grease (uncleaned), the wool either not being washed before weaving or if washed, is re-oiled before being woven. See Chapter 1 for details of the oiling procedure. Incidentally, this oiling process is essential with machine spun wool for the oily nature of the thread gives to tweed much of its characteristic quality.

After weaving tweed cloth is washed lightly, shrunk and stretched a number of times before being made into garments. The general procedure is as follows:

(1) Soak the cloth in hot water for some time.

(2) Place in hot, very soapy solution (110 degree to 120 degrees Fahrenheit) and well worked, preferably by treading with the feet.

(3) The next stage is milling which is carried out with a minimum of water but large quantities of soap which is applied most conveniently in the form of pure soap flakes. A note of caution is needed here. Tweed as such will be completely ruined if treated with anything other than the purest and mildest of soaps. Soda solutions and detergents and in particular dry cleaning, must not be applied to tweed as the essential tweed quality is largely dependent on the retention of some oil in the material.

(4) To mill, the cloth is folded in a zig-zag fashion with soap flakes spread between the folds, laid on a firm surface and trodden until the finish is obtained.

(5) The milled cloth is well rinsed in several changes of soft water and with the assistance of several helpers, pulled into shape while still damp. As a matter of interest, this whole process is known as 'waulking'.

(6) The still damp cloth is finally spread onto a drying frame being pulled flat and straight in the process. This drying process sets the cloth and subsequent pressing should not be necessary.

Homespun, hand woven, home treated tweeds are aristocratic materials and most rewarding cloth to make, for no machine made cloth-making process can duplicate the inherent quality of the hand-made article.

Conclusion

It is fitting perhaps that this book should conclude with a small section on one of the most valuable products of the home weaver's craft. The endeavour has been to impart sufficient understanding of weaving and spinning to allow for each weaver developing to the full their own inherent ability for self-expression. To work and create remains an essential part of a well balanced and healthy mental and physical life. It is hoped that this book may assist readers towards achieving the satisfaction of creativity in the art/craft of spinning and weaving.